The Natural Hygiene Handbook

American Natural Hygiene Society, Inc.

The Natural Hygiene Handbook

From the Editors of *Health Science* Magazine

American Natural Hygiene Society, Inc.

The Natural Hygiene Handbook
First Edition 1996

©1996 American Natural Hygiene Society, Inc. All rights reserved. This book may not be reproduced in whole or in part by any means without permission of the publisher:

American Natural Hygiene Society, Inc.
P.O. Box 30630, Tampa, FL 33630

Appreciation:
We want to thank everyone who has shared articles, personal experiences, and other expertise in *Health Science* magazine. It is from this body of knowledge and experience that *The Natural Hygiene Handbook* was compiled.

Editors:
James Michael Lennon and Susan Taylor

Copy Editors:
Linda Grudnik and Terry Kennedy

ISBN 0-914532-40-5
Library of Congress Catalog Number: 96-86830

PRINTED IN THE UNITED STATES OF AMERICA

Printed on Recycled Paper

▼ ▼ ▼ ▼ ▼ ▼ ▼ ▼ ▼ ▼ ▼

Special Thanks

The publication of this book was made possible by a grant from the James Hervey Johnson Charitable Educational Trust.

James Hervey Johnson (1901-1988) was an active member of the American Natural Hygiene Society. His legacy of commitment to Natural Hygiene spans the decades to the present day.

Mr. Johnson was active for many years and held office in the Society's local chapter in San Diego. In 1963, he was the chairman and host of the Society's ANHS International Natural Living Conference in his hometown of San Diego, Calif.

The American Natural Hygiene Society gratefully thanks the James Hervey Johnson Charitable Educational Trust, Bonnie Lange and Kevin Munnelly, Trustees, for helping the Society spread Mr. Johnson's health views—Natural Hygiene, the science of health.

Publisher's Note

This book describes an approach to healthful living that has had beneficial effects for the many thousands of people who have implemented it during the past 150 years.

Nothing in this handbook is intended to constitute medical treatment or advice of any nature. Moreover, as every person responds differently to diet and lifestyle modification, it is strongly recommended that any person desiring to make dramatic changes in his or her diet or lifestyle consult with his or her physician.

▼ ▼ ▼ ▼ ▼ ▼ ▼ ▼ ▼ ▼ ▼

Acknowledgements

We acknowledge our indebtedness to all of the people who have contributed to *Health Science* magazine over the years, upon whose expertise, experience, and observations the information and opinions in this handbook have been based.

We would especially like to thank: Alec Burton, M.Sc., D.O., D.C,. and Nejla Burton, D.O., D.C., of Australia; Alan Goldhamer, D.C., Ronald G. Cridland, M.D., David Engle, D.C., Alec Isabeau, D.C., Erwin Linzner, D.C., Jennifer Marano, D.C., and Susan Smith Jones, Ph.D., of California; Philip Martin, D.C., of Canada; Keki Sidhwa, N.D., D.O., of England; Frank Sabatino, D.C., Ph.D., of Florida; Paula Duvall of Indiana; Joel Fuhrman, M.D., of New Jersey; Joy Gross of New York; D.J. Scott, D.C., of Ohio; and Ralph C. Cinque, D.C., of Texas.

We want to thank Drs. Gerald Benesh of California and William Esser of Florida—the two surviving co-founders of the American Natural Hygiene Society—for their vision and compassionate support.

This project could not have reached fruition without the ongoing support of the Board of Directors of the American Natural Hygiene Society: Mark A. Huberman, President; David Engle, D.C., Vice President; Dorothy Brosious, Treasurer; Meg Friedrich, Secretary; Ronald G. Cridland, M.D.; Gerald Deutsch; Mark Epstein; Joel Fuhrman, M.D.; Pamela Gerry; Harold Hoffman; Jean Oswald; Daniel Regan; and Roslyn Reynolds-Brescia.

We thank Bud Grudnik of House of Graphics and David Creamer of I.D.E.A.S. for their graphic design and technical support; and Sidney Harris for his insightful cartoons.

Dedication

We dedicate this book to the men and women who during the past 150 years have dedicated their lives to carrying the vital message of Natural Hygiene to people around the world. By their numerous efforts, large and small, these men and women have marked themselves as leaders of the great and noble work of building a healthier and happier world for everyone, everywhere.

Table of Contents

	Introduction	*11*
1.	Who Should Read This Book?	13
2.	Benefits You Get from Natural Hygiene	19
3.	History of Natural Hygiene	31
4.	Natural Hygiene Diet	39
5.	Designing a Diet That's Right for You	49
6.	Food Combining Made Easier	61
7.	Sleep and Your Health	67
8.	The Benefits of Exercise	71
9.	Creating Your Healthful Environment	77
10.	Being Different with Style	81
11.	The Benefits of Fasting	89
12.	Frequently Asked Questions	99
13.	Natural Hygiene Resources	105
14.	Natural Hygiene Books and Tapes	113
15.	Physicians in Natural Hygiene	119
16.	Becoming an ANHS Member	125

▼ ▼ ▼ ▼ ▼ ▼ ▼ ▼ ▼ ▼ ▼

Introduction

Natural Hygiene is a timeless approach to health and happiness that has helped to transform the lives of countless thousands of people. It focuses on common-sense practices that can help you lead the healthiest, happiest life possible.

Natural Hygiene teaches you how to effectively manage all aspects of a healthful lifestyle—diet; exercise; rest and sleep; home and work environment; stress management; and psychology—and offers guidelines to help you live in harmony with Nature.

The premise of Natural Hygiene is that *health is normal*—the way we ought to be all the time. It also recognizes that *healing is a biological process,* and that your body is capable of defending, regulating, and healing itself, if given the proper conditions.

The *Natural Hygiene Handbook* will tell you how to maximize your health to the fullest extent possible. It will motivate you to start and *maintain* a healthful lifestyle. This *Handbook* also will explain the tenets of the American Natural Hygiene Society—an extraordinary organization that can help offer you a support system while you are making changes.

The American Natural Hygiene Society has promoted the principles and practices of Natural Hygiene for almost 50 years. This *Handbook* will give you an introduction to the most up-to-date information about an enormously successful system of health—Natural Hygiene—that dates back more than 150 years.

Offering simple, practical guidelines for better health, this *Handbook* includes information on diet and nutrition; delicious recipes; exercise; rest and sleep; health and well-being; recovery of health; and so much more! Plus you will find information on Natural Hygiene books, audiotapes, and videotapes; and a helpful chapter on the most commonly asked questions about Natural Hygiene.

Welcome to a new life of unprecedented health and vitality. Be prepared to begin experiencing a richer, more enjoyable, and more fulfilling life than you ever dreamed possible!

1

Who Should Read This Book?

Everyone who cares about their health—and the health of their loved ones—should read this book today! Your life depends on learning how to live healthfully. It is estimated that more than 800,000 Americans die prematurely every year from diseases they could have avoided by changing their diets and lifestyles.

You don't have to be one of them!

This handbook is designed to change your life forever! It will provide you with powerful health information that will empower you to live a healthier, happier life than you ever thought possible! And it will help you avoid the premature suffering and death (and financial ruin for you and your family) that conventional living brings to so many of us.

What you will learn

This handbook will teach you new and incredibly powerful concepts about natural weight loss; the dramatic benefits of a plant-based diet; how to get the most out

Each year more than 800,000 people in America die from preventable diseases!

Take charge of your own health!

of exercise without overdoing it; fasting for health and rejuvenation; why you can never reach optimal health or longevity without sufficient rest and sleep; the importance of pure water, fresh air, and sunshine; why it is so important to develop the social skills necessary to live healthfully in an unhealthful world; and more.

You will learn everything you need to know to begin living the life of your dreams. Say goodbye to weight problems, headaches, digestive problems, and fatigue; plus dramatically reduce your risk of the major killers in America—heart disease and cancer!

Health care is self-care!

What's more, you will achieve all this *on your own*, without dependence on anyone else. Natural Hygiene teaches you the most important health principle you will ever learn—health care is *self-care!* Living in a way that builds and restores health is the key. This easy-to-use handbook will help you reclaim the power over your own health destiny.

Health cannot be bought

Key idea! ➡ Health is not something you can buy! You can only *create it* for yourself. This handbook will introduce you to true health independence for the first time in your life! You will learn vitally important, practical information from eminent Hygienic physicians and other qualified teachers that will enable you to begin to take control of your *own* health to the greatest degree possible—whenever and wherever you want.

Timeless teachings

Natural Hygiene is an extraordinary health and wellness program. For more than 150 years, Natural Hygiene has continuously evolved and has helped millions of people of all ages maximize their health potential. It is a comprehensive system of easy-to-understand principles and practices.

A totally unique health system

No other health system compares with Natural Hygiene. It is unique in two ways. It is the only *genuinely* natural health strategy, and it is the only health system that bases its practices entirely on *scientific* principles.

100% natural!

The typical supplements, protein powders, herbal extracts, energy "enhancers," internal "cleansers," appetite suppressants, and other quick-fix "remedies" that domi-

No need for any pills, powders, or potions!

"Take some antibodies and call me in the morning."

nate the "alternative health" field are nowhere to be found in Natural Hygiene. Instead, you will receive practical, no-nonsense advice on how to live an exquisitely beautiful and rewarding life, without having to depend on the latest health fad.

You deserve the best!

Learn what your true health needs are!

Natural Hygiene will give you an in-depth understanding of your true health needs—fresh whole foods, exercise, rest and sleep, fresh air, pure water, sunshine, self-esteem, and healthy relationships—and teach you how to use them to maximize your *individual* health potential.

The reason Natural Hygiene can claim to be the only health philosophy based on scientific principles is that

"We're hoping for a major breakthrough which will be a boon to mankind and will provide our stockholders with a substantial return on their investments."

no other system universally bases its practices on the fact that healing is a biological process, and that health is the result of healthful living.

◂ *Key ideas!*

Powerfully life-affirming

Natural Hygiene is a manifestation of a deep and profound love for life—a love that encompasses ourselves, our families and friends; a love that encompasses all people and all living things, including Earth herself. It recognizes the unity of all life and holds that personal health, environmental health, and community health are parts of a whole, and that no one of these will ever be fully achieved until all are achieved.

You have probably already noticed the interconnectedness of health and wealth. Almost everyone recognizes that wealth depends on health—that even the richest man is miserable when he has a toothache.

Likewise, none of us can be healthy if the environment in which we live is unhealthy. So it behooves even the rich and powerful to be good caretakers of the environment. Where will they build their palatial estates if industrial and corporate greed destroy the air, water, soil, forests, and other elements that make our planet so wondrous and beautiful?

A new way of seeing health and health care

This handbook will open the door to a revolutionary new vision of health and hope. It describes the possibility of a beautiful and bountiful planet inhabited by people with open minds guided by loving hearts. Natural Hygiene is a positive philosophy, and those of us who practice it become great optimists. But we also become great realists. We understand that we must take practical steps every day of our lives to achieve our full potential.

The longest journey begins with a first step. Take that step now by making a commitment to being all you can be! Start today on the road to health and happiness for you and your loved ones!

▼ ▼ ▼ ▼ ▼

In the next chapter, you will learn the basic principles of Natural Hygiene and the tremendous benefits you get in building and maintaining health.

2

The Benefits You Get From Natural Hygiene

Never before in history has there been so much interest in the time-honored system of health and happiness known as *Natural Hygiene*.

People everywhere are fascinated by the possibility of maximizing their health to a degree unimaginable in the day-to-day, conventional world. They are irresistibly attracted by the promise of a vibrant, high-energy life, free from the aches and pains, common ailments, and diseases that are all too common today. People want to get these benefits, and they are ready to take stock of themselves and begin building a life truly worth living.

← Discover your full health potential!

Natural Hygiene teaches us how to understand our relationship with the world—our relationship with the environment and with other people. Its principles guide us in a world where circumstances are not always ideal or sympathetic. These principles give us great strength and the ability to take the steps necessary to secure the optimum life possible with the choices open to us.

For more than a century, Natural Hygienists have

been addressing the full spectrum of health. They rank among the all too few who understand that personal health, environmental health, and community health are parts of a whole.

Taking control of your life

The beauty of Natural Hygiene is that it teaches you how to use the lifestyle variables under your control in a way that brings about extraordinary health and happiness. Learning about Natural Hygiene is a great way of turning self-limiting thinking—such as "I'll just have to learn to live with it," and "What should I expect at my age?"—into hope and optimism. Natural Hygiene can empower you to take the steps necessary to achieve previous-

"We've run the whole gamut of tests on you, and you now appear to be suffering from overtesting."

ly undreamed of health, recovery, and well-being. The effort necessary to make these changes is well worth it!

Growing up, most of us were taught an outdated and thoroughly unscientific way of looking at health and disease. Natural Hygiene gives you an entirely new outlook, by teaching you how your body really works. Once you know that, you are well on your way to a life of health and freedom, instead of one of fear and illness.

A new outlook on health!

To get the benefits of Natural Hygiene, you will need to throw away all of the self-limiting ideas about health and disease that you have learned from those who benefit from your fear, your bad diet and lifestyle choices, and, ultimately, your illnesses and premature death.

Natural Hygiene can be defined as a philosophy based on science, and as a system of principles that help us decide what actions we should take in order to maximize health. These principles have been developed and refined through study and observation, utilizing the power of the scientific method. Science helps us tell the difference between fact and fantasy. Unlike medicine and most other health philosophies, which focus on the diagnosis and treatment of disease, Natural Hygiene is concerned with the principles that underlie health.

Some basic principles of Natural Hygiene

Although some of its recommendations are similar to those of other health systems, Natural Hygiene is unique in its contention that:

1. Health is normal.

For most people, health is as simple as living in harmony with Nature. Your body is self-generating, self-regulating, and self-repairing. You started out as the minute union of two cells in your mother's womb; you developed into a child, and later grew into adulthood. All that time your body has been going about its business, night and day, winter and summer, in sickness and in health, without too much help. Your body's capacities for growth, repair, and maintenance are a manifestation of an extraordinary intelligence. Learn to read your body's signs and heed its warnings.

2. Health and disease are a continuum.

Key ➡ idea!

The same physiological laws govern life in sickness and in health. Sick persons use the same practices, modified if necessary, to recover health that healthy persons use to maintain it.

3. Health results from healthful living.

Health care is, for the most part, *self-care.* To be healthy, we need to live healthfully every day—develop self-esteem and a positive attitude towards life; eat fresh, whole natural foods; exercise regularly; get plenty of rest and sleep; get plenty of fresh air and sunshine; learn to handle stress; and avoid all of the negative influences of life.

Key ➡ idea!

People can become sick from either inadequate intake of essential nutrients or from excess intake of nutrients. In the industrialized nations, much more disease is caused by excess of nutrients—especially excess fat and protein. The most common causes of death and debility—including coronary artery disease; stroke; diabetes; emphysema; cancer

"You're suffering from an overdose of vitamin C. I'm going to give you some common cold virus to combat it."

of the lung, colon, breast, and prostate; kidney disease; osteoporosis, and autoimmune diseases—are associated with excess intake of calories in general, and consumption of animal fat and protein in particular.

These conditions of excess nutrition do not respond particularly well to conventional medical treatments. To recover, people with these conditions must eliminate their excesses. They need to make radical dietary changes—eliminating the use of meat, fish, fowl, eggs, dairy products, oil, and excess salt and sugar, and eating a diet consisting of fresh fruits and vegetables, whole grains, and legumes. Correction of their real deficiencies—typically sleep, exercise, and fiber intake—also will be of critical importance.

4. Healing is a biological process.

Key idea! ➡ Except in extraordinary circumstances, healing is the result of actions undertaken by the body on its own behalf. There are times when assistance, including medical treatment and surgery, is necessary. But recovery ultimately is dependent upon biological processes.

5. The causes of disease must be removed.

Key idea! ➡ Natural Hygienists recognize that there is a big difference between the *symptoms* of disease—such as fever, inflammation, diarrhea, vomiting, and mucus discharge—and the *causes* of the symptoms, which could include overindulgence or poor choice of food, overwork, exhaustion, and inability to manage stress. The body is self-healing, and the symptoms associated with acute disease that are generated by the body may be important processes that are needed for efficient healing to take place. The suppression of these symptoms may have negative, and even dire, consequences.

Health is much more than the absence of symptoms. In fact, the belief that health is the absence of symptoms is dangerous. When we suppress symptoms without eliminating the underlying causes, we run a terrible risk. The problem(s) may seem to have been solved, but in the end a steep price may have to be paid for failing to see the connection between our destructive behavior and its consequences. This connection is often difficult to recognize because the human body can compensate for enormous amounts of abuse before breaking down.

To recover health, we must remove the causes of disease, allow time for the body to respond to the causes, and avoid the common mistake of trying to suppress symptoms.

6. *The body functions as a unit.*
For the most part, there can never be partial health or partial (meaning "singular") disease. There is a unity of the body. Every part has a function. If one part

"Let's see now..."

starts to malfunction, it affects the whole person.

7. *Emotional factors can effect health.*
Immeasurable damage can be done by worry, fear, suspicion, jealousy, hate, and other destructive emotions. Many bodily functions can be affected.

Strong advocacy for a healthful world
Over the years, the American Natural Hygiene Society (ANHS) has taken strong leadership positions on many important issues, including:

1. Promoting vegetarianism for nearly 50 years
In addition to being the oldest and largest Natural

"Well, my lawyer says I have to check your blood pressure."

Hygiene organization in the world, ANHS is the oldest vegetarian organization in the United States. Natural Hygienists have advocated vegetarianism for more than 150 years, for reasons of personal and public health, responsible land use, and compassion for other sentient beings.

2. Advocates freedom of choice in health care
ANHS supports health freedom—your right to choose whatever form of health care you wish, including the right to accept or reject any or all treatment. ANHS strongly opposes *compulsory* treatments or procedures of any kind—including compulsory inoculation, fluoridation of water, and forced blood tests or X rays—under all circumstances, as a matter of science, safety, and conscience.

We hold that individuals have an inalienable right to enjoy the same freedom from government-sponsored health programs that they enjoy from government-sponsored religion. Likewise, we are united in opposition to the establishment of a medical/pharmaceutical monopoly which dictates the control of national health policies.

3. Supports organic food movement
ANHS strongly supports the organic food movement, and opposes the chemicalization of our food supply. We strongly oppose food irradiation on grounds of both environmental and food safety.

4. Supports environmental protection
Natural Hygienists have long supported the envi-

ronmental movement. We insist that laws be enforced to compel industrial conglomerates to cease poisoning our air, soil, and water with pollutants. Destruction of the environment for commercial ends is a tragic example of bad business practice. The environment is the place from which all other material wealth is derived.

We support all efforts to protect the delicate balance of nature by preserving our natural resources, recycling our wastes, protecting our endangered wildlife, and developing alternative sources of energy, especially solar energy.

5. Advocates a smoke-free environment
We believe that everyone has a right to a smoke-free environment. We urge that smoking prohibitions be strictly enforced and extended to include all public facilities, governmental institutions, and modes of public transportation.

6. Warns about the hazards of radiation
We believe that freedom from the hazards of radiation is an inherent right. We support efforts to abolish or limit the cancer-causing emissions from potentially harmful sources, such as nuclear reactors and weapons, food and medical irradiation plants, microwave transmissions, high voltage wires, and medical and dental X rays.

Committed to a healthful world
Natural Hygienists will always support efforts that protect the environment, safeguard our natural resources,

"Apparently the pesticides in your diet are down, while the pesticides in the air you breathe are up, and the pesticides in your drinking water remain the same."

and improve the health and quality of life for people everywhere, including all future generations.

Great personal freedom

Natural Hygiene is a philosophy based on science. It is an honest look at the world. It makes no exceptions for custom or tradition, however venerable or long-standing. It offers each of us an opportunity to be all we can be, and offers us freedom from our limiting habits of thought, word, and deed.

We can choose to stay prisoners of our accustomed habits, harmful and limiting though they are, or we can choose personal growth and freedom. Natural Hygiene gives us the tools and information necessary to choose wisely and successfully.

Health excellence ➡

When thinking about Natural Hygiene, one of the first words that comes to mind is "excellence," because Natural Hygiene gives us a tremendous opportunity to be all we can be. It is a philosophy for people who are looking for the good life—and not just a *pretty* good life, but a *very* good life!

▼ ▼ ▼ ▼ ▼

In the next chapter, you will learn about the remarkable history of Natural Hygiene.

3

History of Natural Hygiene

Natural Hygiene has a long and impressive history. Much of the health and nutrition advice being touted today as "new" and "revolutionary"—such as the advantages of a vegetarian diet, the incredible self-healing powers of the body, the role of fasting in the recovery of health, and the importance of avoiding unnecessary drugs and surgery—were promoted by Natural Hygienists as far back as 150 years ago.

Leading the health movement for over 150 years!

Beginning in the 1830s, the Hygiene Movement has been led by an unbroken line of physicians who rejected orthodox medical practice and dedicated themselves to teaching people how to live disease-free lives. These men and women were startlingly ahead of their times.

Pioneers of Natural Hygiene

Some of the most prominent among these physicians were: Isaac Jennings, M.D. (1788-1874); William Alcott, M.D. (1798-1859) (cousin of Louisa May Alcott); James Caleb Jackson, M.D. (1811-1895); Russell Thacker Trall,

M.D. (1812-1877);Thomas Low Nichols, M.D. (1815-1901); George H. Taylor, M.D. (1821-1896); Harriet Austin, M.D. (1826-1891); Susanna Way Dodds, M.D. (1830-1911); Emmett Densmore, M.D. (1837-1911); Robert Walter, M.D. (1841-1921); Felix Oswald, M.D. (1845-1906); John Tilden, M.D. (1851-1940); George S. Weger, M.D. (1874-1935); and Herbert M. Shelton, N.D. (1895-1985).

A bad time to get sick

If you got sick in the early 1800s, you were a candidate for such barbaric "care" as: bleeding (drawing blood from you); applying leeches directly on your skin; blistering, burning, and cauterizing (to "draw" the pain away); forced purging and vomiting; and, of course, taking highly-toxic

The 'cures' were worse than the diseases!

"I stopped taking the medicine because I prefer the original disease to the side effects."

(and long since abandoned) drugs. Water was routinely withheld from the sick, heightening your chances of dying from dehydration. The death rate was quite high, and the illness recovery rate was quite low.

Pork, white bread, and lard pies predominated in diets, while fruits and vegetables were looked down upon. Bathing was infrequent, and buildings were closed up tightly against sunshine and "night" air, which was considered poisonous. Sanitation was lacking, tobacco was widely used, and alcohol was the favorite beverage.

← A diet hard to swallow!

A new approach to health

By contrast, Hygienic advice at the time consisted of adequate fresh air, sunshine, bathing, cleanliness, sufficient rest and sleep, and whole natural foods—except in sickness, when abstinence was sometimes recommended.

Hygienic physicians observed that patients who for one reason or another did not take their prescribed drugs recovered more quickly and satisfactorily than those who did. This inspired them to explore the self-healing mechanisms of the body, and the health and lifestyle factors that supported them. They quickly discovered that health was the result of healthful living. Except in unusual circumstances, all one had to do to preserve a state of health and to prevent disease was to supply the essentials of health to the body.

Drugs were not the answer!

Women in Hygiene

Women were a vital part of the Hygienic Movement. In 1852, Russell Trall, M.D., established a school based on Hygienic principles, the New York Hygeio-Therapeutic College, in New York City. Men and women were admit-

The first women physicians!

ted on an equal basis. The first women physicians in America graduated from this school, including Harriet Austin, M.D., a close friend of Clara Barton, and Mary Walker, M.D. (1832-1919). Dr. Walker, who was a champion of women's causes, served in the Civil War and was the first (and only) woman to receive the Congressional Medal of Honor.

Mary Gove (1810-1884) and Susanna Way Dodds, M.D., also founded colleges that taught Hygiene and admitted both men and women. Gove and her husband, Thomas Low Nichols, M.D., established the American Hydropathic Institute in New York City in 1851. Dr. Dodds, together with her sister-in-law, Mary Dodds,

"There could be any number of causes for this condition. Perhaps he broke a mirror or walked under a ladder or spilled some salt..."

M.D., founded the Hygienic College of Physicians and Surgeons in St. Louis, Mo. in 1887. Harriot Austin, M.D.

Dodds, Gove, and Austin were at the forefront of sex education for women and children, human rights, women's rights, and clothing reform for women. The clothes worn by women of that period were horrific. Stiff whalebone corsets and long dresses inhibited breathing and greatly restricted movement. Even before the Civil War, Austin and Dodds were advocating and wearing slacks as a matter both of health and equality. (Gove wore bloomers.) Gove also spoke out against slavery and the marriage laws of the period that denied women many basic rights.

Sex education and women's rights!

The profound influence of Natural Hygiene

By the end of the 19th century, Hygienic principles had found their way into American life, and, to some extent, into prescribed medical practice. This health revolution saw the adoption of exercise, sunbathing, ventilated homes and offices, better modes of clothing, fruits and vegetables in greater abundance, and improved sanitary practices.

Hygiene starts health revolution that is still alive today!

Improved bathing and sanitation led to a dramatic decrease in many diseases common to the period. As a result, the term Hygiene (which means "the science of health") became corrupted and reduced in popular language to mean "cleanliness" of one sort or another.

Hygiene means more than cleanliness!

In the mid-1900s, Herbert Shelton, N.D., undertook the monumental task of reviewing and updating the writings of previous generations of Hygienic physicians so that the information would be consistent with the scientific knowledge of his day.

The learning continues

As the science of health, Natural Hygiene is driven by science and scientific thinking. As our knowledge of the physical and psychological needs of human beings changes and grows, Natural Hygiene changes and grows.

The "timeless" aspects of Natural Hygiene are its basic principles, of which "health is the result of healthful living," and "healing is a biological process" are foremost. These principles seem almost self-evident to those of us reading them today, but they were once considered radical and revolutionary.

The following quotes will give you an idea of how long Natural Hygienists have been heralding the life-saving message that "health care is self-care."

Key idea! ➡ "Man is so constituted and organized, and is so related to the external world, that if he will obey the laws of his being he may live free from sickness and the fear of premature death, and may attain to a high degree of physical strength and beauty.

"But there can be no law without penalty; and pain, sickness, sorrow, deformity, decrepitude, and untimely death are the direct and legitimate results of the violation of physical law."

James C. Jackson, M.D. (1811-1895)

Key idea! ➡ "The system which we endorse and practice is true—in harmony with nature, in accordance with the laws of the vital organism, correct in science, sound in philosophy, in agreement with common sense, successful in results, and a blessing to mankind."

Russell Thacker Trall, M.D. (1812-1877)

"The people need to learn that the natural condition of human beings is one of health; and that every instance of sickness and suffering, unless caused by accident, is caused by some wrong doing, either on

"Your problem is that the seven drugs which you're taking are cancelling each other out."

the part of the sufferer or others."

Harriet Austin, M.D. (1826-1891)

"Life is lengthened and filled with joy by living in accordance with nature's teachings. It is not only shortened but rendered miserable and worthless by pursuing an opposite course."

Susanna Way Dodds, M.D. (1830-1915)

"Health represents a body and mind adjusted to, and in unison with, the laws of nature. And disease represents any departure from this ideal state."

John H. Tilden, M.D. (1851-1940)

"You cannot remain or become strong through exercise alone, or diet alone, or rest and sleep alone. Fresh air and sunshine alone are not enough. Do not imagine that by [correct] breathing alone you can reach the heights. All these things are good, but life is more than exercise, or food and drink; more

⬅ *Key idea!*

than thought, or rest and sleep. It is all these and more. Life must be lived as a whole."

Herbert M. Shelton, N.D. (1895-1985)

Natural Hygiene in the 21st century

In 1985, an extraordinary book, *Fit For Life,* by Harvey and Marilyn Diamond, became the best-selling diet and health book in history. It introduced 11 million people to the American Natural Hygiene Society, ushering in a new era for Natural Hygiene.

Oldest Natural Hygiene organization in the world!

Founded in 1948, the American Natural Hygiene Society is at the forefront of bringing the timeless principles and the most accurate and up-to-date information about Natural Hygiene into the next century. Through its journal, *Health Science* magazine, and its International Natural Living Conferences and regional seminars, the Society presents articles and lectures by the members of the International Association of Hygienic Physicians, who continue to bring new information and new perspectives into the arena of Hygienic living and health care.

The Society is as committed to furthering the ideas and practices that can reform the health of our country as were the Hygienic pioneers of the 1830s. At a time when millions of people are suffering needlessly, the voice of Natural Hygiene remains strong—and offers much needed hope to the world.

▼ ▼ ▼ ▼ ▼

In the next chapter, you will learn the powerful, yet easy to understand, basics of the Natural Hygiene Diet!

4

Natural Hygiene Diet

For more than 150 years, Natural Hygienists have advocated the avoidance of animal products—meat, fish, fowl, eggs, and dairy products. In fact, the American Natural Hygiene Society has been promoting a vegetarian diet longer (since 1948) than any other health organization in the United States.

By sharp contrast, the medical establishment has only recently, and reluctantly, begun to acknowledge the inseparable relationship between diet and health. Medicine has long recognized that deficiencies can cause disease, but only recently has dietary *excess* been acknowledged as a significant factor in the evolution of numerous degenerative diseases such as heart disease, cancer, diabetes, osteoporosis, and kidney disease.

Dietary excess is a significant factor in many diseases.

Contrary to what the food supplement industry would like you to think, diseases from nutritional deficiency are not nearly as common as degenerative diseases from dietary excess. The major deficiency most Americans should be concerned about is the lack of fiber in their diets, since they don't eat enough fruits, vegetables, whole grains, and legumes. Meat and dairy products do not contain any fiber, and foods made from refined grains—such as white bread, white rice, and white pasta—have had their fiber removed.

Lack of dietary fiber increases your risk of cancer!

Fiber deficiency leads to many common health problems such as constipation, hemorrhoids, varicose veins, hiatus hernia, and hypoglycemia. Lack of fiber in the diet makes diabetes much harder to control, and is a major factor in increasing the incidence of cancer, especially colon and breast cancer.

Science supports vegetarian diet

The bulk of the scientific literature overwhelmingly supports the Hygienic contention that human beings function best on a diet derived from whole natural foods including fruits, vegetables, whole grains, and legumes—a diet that excludes animal products.

A diet derived exclusively from whole, natural foods provides you with the both the quantity and quality of nutrients you need for optimum health, so long as you eat enough to meet your individual caloric needs.

Whole, natural foods provide all of the nutrients you need in abundance!

These nutrients include *protein* (for its essential amino acid components), *fat* (for its essential fatty acid components), *complex carbohydrates* (as a clean-burning source of fuel), *vitamins* (for their role as catalysts and cofactors), *minerals* (that serve as structural components), *fiber* (as a necessary source of roughage), *water* (the universal solvent), and *phytochemicals* (for the possible role they play in supporting and protecting the body).

On the specific issue of protein—a healthful, calorie-sufficient, whole-food, plant-based diet will supply ample amounts of high-quality protein per day.

Problems with eating animal products

Unlike other animals that include meat in their diet, humans are unable to break down uric acid. This is due to the fact that we do not possess the necessary enzyme, uricase. This inability to break down uric acid leads to an increased possibility of its accumulating in the body when animal products are eaten. Uric acid is an intermediary product of metabolism that is associated with various pathological states, including gout.

> Human beings are not designed for a diet based on meat!

The human liver, unlike the livers of carnivores, can only process a limited amount of cholesterol. If significant amounts of animal products are consumed, cholesterol levels rise, along with an increased risk of developing atherosclerosis. Clearly, the human liver was not designed to handle the large amounts of animal products that are consumed by most Americans.

Uncooked or improperly cooked meat, fish, fowl, and dairy products are the source of parasites and contamination—such as trichinosis (found in pork and pork-contaminated beef) and salmonellosis (found in chicken, milk products, and other contaminated animal products).

The price we pay for meat

Vegetarians use fewer healthcare services and spend less time in hospitals than people who eat meat.

Eating meat can cost you big— your money and your life!

Most of us know how much a hamburger costs at the local fast-food joint, but few of us realize how much meat eating costs Americans in annual healthcare costs.

According to a report published in the November, 1995 issue of *Preventive Medicine,* meat eating results in as much as $61 *billion* in annual healthcare costs due to increases in heart disease, hypertension, cancer, diabetes, gallstones, obesity-related problems, and food-borne illness.

Meat eaters also are more likely to smoke and drink alcohol, further jeopardizing their health. The medical costs attributable to smoking are generally considered to be $50 billion annually.

Vegetarian diet now on Uncle Sam's menu

The scientific support for vegetarianism is now so strong that even the government of the United States has had to recognize the nutritional adequacy of both the vegetarian and vegan [totally free of animal products] diets. This came in the wake of the nearly 50 years of pressure from the American Natural Hygiene Society and other health groups.

In 1995, the government publication *Dietary Guidelines for Americans*—the nation's blueprint for nutrition programs, which is updated every five years—not only gave its stamp of approval to the vegetarian and vegan diets, but also stated that a healthful diet can help reduce the risks of developing diseases such as heart disease, certain cancers, diabetes, stroke, and osteoporosis, as well as reduce major risk factors such as obesity, high blood pressure, and high cholesterol.

United States government recognizes vegetarian and vegan diets!

More progress still needed

While the U.S. government has made progress in its *Dietary Guidelines for Americans,* its recommendations still show the influence of industry groups who want their products included in this influential publication. As a result, parts of the *Dietary Guidelines* look as much like a fast-food menu as they do a scientific document.

◀ Dietary guidelines in debate!

The government's *Food Guide Pyramid,* which is included in the *Dietary Guidelines,* still recommends two to three servings of meat and two to three servings of dairy products every day, in spite of the fact that research shows that avoiding such products is safer than consuming them.

Under the auspices of the Washington-based Physicians Committee for Responsible Medicine, a distinguished group of scientists and physicians has called for the government's meat- and dairy-based diet to be traded for a plant-based diet.

These physicians included Dr. Benjamin Spock, author of *Baby and Child Care,* which has long been the leading guide for parents; Dr. Henry Heimlich, inventor of the Heimlich Maneuver and many other medical innovations; Dr. William Castelli, Director of the Framingham Heart Study; Dr. William Roberts, Editor of the *American Journal of Cardiology;* Dr. Dean Ornish, from the University of California at San Francisco; Dr. Peter Wood, of the Stanford Center for Research in Disease Prevention; Dr. Caldwell Esselstyn, Jr., of the Cleveland Clinic's Department of General Surgery; Dr. Frank Oski, Chairman of the Department of Pediatrics at Johns Hopkins University; Dr. Lawrence Kushi, of the University of Minneso-

*"First of all, there are **not** 16 basic food groups."*

ta; Dr. Oliver Alabaster, Director of the Institute for Disease Prevention of the George Washington University Medical Center; Neal D. Barnard, M.D., President of the Physicians Committee for Responsible Medicine; and many others, including members of the International Association of Hygienic Physicians.

Natural Hygiene dietary recommendations

The Natural Hygiene diet is as easy to understand and to adopt as it is beautiful to see and delicious to eat. The American Natural Hygiene Society recommends a plant-based diet derived exclusively from whole natural foods and avoid meat, fish, fowl, eggs, and dairy products, as well as added oil, salt, sugar, and most processed foods.

Plant-based diet is your key to good health!

These recommendations alone would not make the Natural Hygiene diet special. Natural Hygiene stands apart from other vegetarian and vegan diets in that it recommends that you eat a very large portion of your diet uncooked, use a minimum of spices and other stimulants, and center your diet around fruits and vegetables, including complex starches like potatoes and yams, rather than concentrating primarily on grains.

Natural Hygienists are the original "raw food" advocates, pointing to the joys of eating delicious, nutritious meals fresh from nature's bountiful gardens and orchards. ("Food" from slaughterhouses and food processing plants simply cannot compare!) Natural Hygienists recommend simply prepared meals that help discourage overeating, and in the 1930s devised a popular practice known as "food combining" to help people achieve this.

Uncooked fruits and vegetables are alive with exquis-

"It's partly glandular...and partly 8,500 calories per day."

ite flavors and aromas, and provide you with nature's full palate of nutrients (vitamins, minerals, amino acids, phytochemicals, enzymes), fiber, and water in abundance.

Eat *more!* A health-promoting diet is *high* in nutrients and *low* in calories!

Fresh fruits and vegetables are nature's perfect foods, and they are low in calories. Raw salad vegetables—such as leaf lettuce, celery, carrots, tomatoes, sweet red peppers, broccoli, cauliflower, jicama, kohlrabi, snow peas, sweet cabbages, and cucumbers—contain on average only about 100 calories per pound. Fresh fruit—apples, pears, bananas, apricots, plums, nectarines, fresh figs, grapes, peaches, oranges, strawberries, blueberries, raspberries, persimmons, watermelon, cantaloupe, and countless other regional fruit—contains on average only about 300 calories per pound.

If you decided to eat a diet made up of raw fruits and vegetables only, you would need to eat a very large volume of food to get sufficient calories to maintain your weight and energy levels. Because most active adults need about 2,000 calories per day, you would need to eat at least 12 to 15 pounds of fruits and vegetables each day.

Fortunately, steamed vegetables contain on average about 300 calories per pound (and some people find them easier to eat); baked potatoes, yams, and hard squashes contain on average about 500 calories per pound; grains, such as brown rice, millet, and quinoa, also contain about 500 calories per pound; avocados (which are high in fat) contain about 800 calories per pound; and raw, unsalted nuts (which are *very* high in fat) contain about 2,500 calories per pound.

What should I eat?

A good starting point when beginning to eat healthfully is to eat a large volume of fresh, raw fruits and vegetables (three to five pounds per day, yielding 600 to 1,100 calories) and to get enough cooked, starchy vegetables (such as potatoes, yams, and hard squashes) and whole grains and legumes (such as brown rice, millet, quinoa, corn, lentils, and other beans) so that you can maintain good strength and energy levels and not get too skinny.

A large portion of your diet should be uncooked fruits and vegetables!

Because some vegetable foods are naturally high in fat and protein, it makes sense to eat them sparingly. It is recommended that you are careful not to consume large quantities of avocado, nuts, or soy products on a daily basis.

← Important tip!

First things first

It is important to keep the big picture in mind when you start making dietary changes. People just starting out often focus much of their attention on insignificant points. Please don't become one of them!

It is all too common to hear people who have never previously given a moment's thought to health or nutrition become instant experts on "live foods," "depleted soils," "enzymes," "food combining," "supplements," etc., minutes after first hearing about them.

Key idea! ➡ The most important step you can take to improve your diet is to eliminate or at least dramatically reduce your consumption of animal products—meat, fish, fowl, eggs, and dairy products. Improving the American diet—including a dramatic reduction or elimination of animal products—could save as many as 300,000 lives each year.

No other dietary change can produce such extraordinary benefits. Eliminate animal products from your diet *now*. Later on, you can argue all you want about minute, theoretical details.

One of the most important concepts that you will ever learn about diet and nutrition is that food is *fuel*. It is so very important that you eat to live and not live to eat.

▼ ▼ ▼ ▼ ▼

*In the next chapter, you will learn practical tips on how to design a diet that meets **your** individual needs.*

5

Designing a Healthful Diet That's Right for You

It sometimes seems like everyone you talk to is trying to eat more healthfully. And as the scientific evidence mounts in support of a whole food, plant-based diet, more and more people want to adopt this health-promoting way of eating. But simply understanding the scientific support for your new diet is not always enough to ensure a successful transition.

Most people have questions about making a transition to healthful eating. Here are the six most frequently asked questions:

1. What foods should I eat?
2. What foods should I avoid?
3. Will my new diet meet all of my nutritional needs?
4. Will I enjoy my new diet?
5. How will I feel physically and emotionally?
6. Can I do it?

The answers to these questions are surprisingly easy to understand and put into practice. Once you learn a few simple principles, you will be on your way to a new way of eating that will bring more health and enjoyment than you might ever have imagined!

What's on the main menu?

You have an amazingly wide range of foods to choose from. There are countless varieties of fresh fruits; vegetables; potatoes and hard squashes; whole grains and legumes; and raw, unsalted nuts and seeds. Prepare yourself for a delightful taste adventure as you explore your new way of eating!

Wide range of fresh, tasty foods to choose from!

The list that follows is a sampling of some of the delicious whole, natural foods that will be the heart and soul of your new diet. For a complete description of these foods and their nutritional breakdowns, order a copy of *Dictionary of Natural Foods,* by Dr. William Esser, from the American Natural Hygiene Society. (See address in the "Natural Hygiene Resources" chapter.)

Fresh fruits

Apples, apricots, avocados, bananas, blackberries, blueberries, cantaloupes, fresh dates, elderberries, fresh figs, gooseberries, grapefruits, grapes, mangos, musk melons, nectarines, oranges, peaches, pears, persimmons, pineapples, plums, raspberries, strawberries, tangerines, watermelon, and countless other exotic fruits such as breadfruits, carambolas, cherimoyas, guavas, jackfruits, papayas, sapadillas, sapotes, and soursops.

Fresh vegetables

Salad vegetables—such as broccoli, sweet cabbages, carrots, cauliflower, celery, corn, cucumbers, jicama, kohlrabi, leaf lettuce, sweet red peppers, snow peas, and tomatoes; plus others—such as artichokes, asparagus, beets, brussels sprouts, collards, eggplant, kale, mustard greens, okra, parsnips, rhubarb, rutabaga, spinach, summer squash, turnips, water chestnuts, and zucchini.

Potatoes and hard squashes
Many varieties of potatoes (including new, russet, white, purple, Yukon gold, and yellow Finn), sweet potatoes, yams, pumpkins, acorn squash, butternut squash, and hubbard squash.

Grains and legumes
Barley, buckwheat (kasha), millet, oats, quinoa, brown rice, and wild rice. Chickpeas, cowpeas, green beans, green peas, lentils, lima beans, pigeonpeas, pinto beans, red beans, snap beans, soybeans, and white beans.

Raw, unsalted nuts and seeds
Almonds, black walnuts, cashews, English walnuts, filberts, hickory nuts, macadamias, pecans, pignolias (pine nuts), pistachios, pumpkin seeds, sesame seeds, and sunflower seeds.

"Our best bet is to ignore nutrition completely, and stress the shape, color, noise, and the toy that comes in the box."

What foods should I avoid?

There are several categories of food you need to avoid—animal products (meat, fish, fowl, eggs, and dairy products); most processed foods; added oils, salt, and sugar; and all food additives and chemicals.

Meeting your nutritional needs

Your nutritional needs change during your lifetime!

People come in all shapes and sizes. We each have different metabolisms, different activity levels, different heights and weights, and different ages. We also have our own individual capacities for digestion. Since each of these factors can change during our lifetime, we always need to fashion a diet that meets our *individual* needs.

With this in mind, two sample daily menus are described below, one for a healthy, active female, 25 to 50 years old; another for a healthy, active male, 25 to 50 years old.

Two sample one-day menus

Here is a one-day example of a health-promoting diet for a healthy, active female, 25 to 50 years old:

Breakfast:
Fresh raw fruit salad including a banana, apple, and strawberries along with celery and one ounce each of almonds and raw pumpkin seeds.

Lunch:
Large raw vegetable salad (lettuce, carrot, beets, tomato, alfalfa sprouts, peas, cucumber) with Tomato Avocado Dressing and a large plate of steamed vegetables and baked potato.

Dinner:
Raw vegetable plate (carrot, jicama, celery, cucumber) with steamed vegetables, and Brown Rice-Lentil Stew.
(For recipes, see the end of this chapter.)

"I'm attempting to transmute calcium oxide, copper, gluconate, manganese sulfate, tyrosine, and benzaldehyde into condensed soup."

Here is a one-day example of a health-promoting diet for a healthy, active male, 25 to 50 years old:

Breakfast:
Orange juice smoothie (orange juice, banana, kiwi) and oatmeal with raisins.

Lunch:
Vegetable plate with avocado slices, steamed vegetables, and Potato-Vegetable Soup.

Dinner:
Large raw vegetable salad (lettuce, carrot, beets, tomato, alfalfa sprouts, peas, cucumber with Tomato Avocado Dressing, a large plate of steamed vegetables, and a bowl of Split Pea–Yam Soup over brown rice.
(For recipes, see the end of this chapter.)

If additional calories are required, a fresh mixed

vegetable juice or fresh fruit could be consumed in the afternoon.

The charts on these pages show that the sample daily menus for women and men described in the text are more than adequate to meet your nutritional needs.

This chart shows that the sample daily menu on page 52 for a healthy, active female, age 25 to 50, is more than adequate!

Average daily nutrients from 1700-calorie menu

Nutrient	Amount	RDA %	Nutrient	Amount	RDA %
Calories	1695 Kc	77.0%	Vitamin C	778.5 mg	1297.0%
Protein	59.74 Gm	110.0%	Vitamin E	43.15 mg	539.0%
Histidine	1411 mg	256.0%	Vitamin K	2373 Ug	3651.0%
Isoleucine	2513 mg	386.0%	Pantothenic Acid	8.724 mg	158.0%
Methionine	759.8 mg	178.0%	Chromium	0.2111 mg	168.0%
Phenylalanine	2475 mg	521.0%	Linoleic Acid	5.553 Gm	113.0%
Threonine	2122 mg	471.0%	Magnesium	688.1 mg	245.0%
Tyrosine	1698 mg	357.0%	Potassium	7364 mg	368.0%
Leucine	3735 mg	393.0%	Copper	3.111 mg	138.0%
Lysine	3055 mg	381.0%	Iron	22.25 mg	148.0%
Tryptophan	684.2 mg	273.0%	Phosphorus	1425 mg	178.0%
Valine	2945 mg	453.0%	Manganese	9.885 mg	282.0%
Vitamin A	7447 RE	930.0%	Selenium	0.184 mg	333.0%
Thiamin B_1	1.938 mg	176.0%	Calcium	933.5 mg	116.0%
Riboflavin B_2	2.118 mg	162.0%	Cholesterol	0.0 mg	n/a
Niacin B_3	22.18 mg	147.0%	Carbohydrate	332.5 Gm	120.0%
Pyridoxine B_6	4.964 mg	310.0%	Weight	3004 Gm	n/a
Cobalamin B_{12}	0.0 Ug	0.0%	Dietary Fiber	71.46 Gm	324.0%

Percent of calories from: Protein: 13% Carbohydrate: 73% Fat: 14%

How to enjoy your new diet

How quickly you will enjoy your new diet pretty much depends on you. Some people like to jump into it all at once—and they feel great! For others, making a swift and dramatic dietary change—from a typical American diet to an Hygienic diet—might leave them feeling physically worse and emotionally deprived for a short time.

You may experience withdrawal symptoms from your old diet, and may need time to develop effective strategies to deal with friends and loved ones who feel threatened by the *new* you.

Average daily nutrients from 2500-calorie menu

Nutrient	Amount	RDA %	Nutrient	Amount	RDA %
Calories	2468 Kc	85.0%	Vitamin C	1176 mg	1960.0%
Protein	86.38 Gm	137.0%	Vitamin E	56.75 mg	567.0%
Histidine	1888 mg	272.0%	Vitamin K	2117 Ug	2646.0%
Isoleucine	3322 mg	405.0%	Pantothenic Acid	10.71 mg	194.0%
Methionine	1105 mg	206.0%	Chromium	0.169 mg	135.0%
Phenylalanine	3454 mg	576.0%	Linoleic Acid	5.625 Gm	87.0%
Threonine	2786 mg	491.0%	Magnesium	963.3 mg	275.0%
Tyrosine	2281 mg	380.0%	Potassium	9632 mg	481.0%
Leucine	5186 mg	433.0%	Copper	3.711 mg	164.0%
Lysine	3978 mg	394.0%	Iron	27.32 mg	273.0%
Tryptophan	922.4 mg	292.0%	Phosphorus	2083 mg	260.0%
Valine	3958 mg	483.0%	Manganese	14.98 mg	428.0%
Vitamin A	10144 RE	1014.0%	Selenium	0.248 mg	354.0%
Thiamin B_1	3.479 mg	231.0%	Calcium	1052 mg	131.0%
Riboflavin B_2	2.11 mg	137.0%	Cholesterol	0.0 mg	n/a
Niacin B_3	23.79 mg	125.0%	Carbohydrate	516.6 Gm	142.0%
Pyridoxine B_6	5.539 mg	276.0%	Weight	4366 Gm	n/a
Cobalamin B_{12}	0.0 Ug	0.0%	Dietary Fiber	88.41 Gm	304.0%

Percent of calories from: Protein: 13% Carbohydrate: 79% Fat: 8%

This chart shows that the sample daily menu on page 53 for a healthy, active male, age 25 to 50, is more than adequate!

Only you can decide if you want to make immediate changes, or if you prefer to make changes gradually.

← *Key idea!*

To be successful in dietary transition, you must create your own natural environment as much as possible. The most important place to start is your home. Don't bring fats, oils, salt, sugar, processed foods, or animal products into your home—not even "just for company." If you have these temptations around, you will either give in to them or waste a lot of energy resisting them.

Strategies for success

It is important for you to develop your own set of strategies to support your new, health-promoting lifestyle. Renew your commitment to live healthfully by re-reading the books, listening to the tapes, and watching the videos that inspired you to make your decision. By attending lectures or seminars periodically you can learn new information and reinforce your health-promoting habits.

Build a personal support system for yourself!

Cultivate friends who value their health and happiness. Pursue activities and interests that give you a feeling of productivity and emotional nourishment.

Key idea ➡

Stop looking to food for more than it can provide. Remember, food is fuel. Eat to live; don't live to eat.

Menu and recipe ideas to help you get started

The bottom line is that what you should be eating—meal after meal, day after day, for *life*—is a wide variety of fresh fruits and vegetables, steamed vegetables, cooked starches (such as potatoes, yams, hard squashes, brown rice, millet, and quinoa). Small servings of naturally rich, high-fat vegetable foods—such as raw, unsalted nuts and avocados—can also be used in moderation.

The most important thing to keep in mind is that you should eat large enough portions of food to meet your caloric needs. You also need to be careful not to eat so much fruit, nuts, and avocados that you end up trading in a high-sugar, high-fat, conventional diet for a high-sugar, high-fat, "natural" diet.

If you are just starting out, you may want to prepare these foods in a way that mimics your more familiar recipes—soups, stews, and casseroles. There are many recipe books available from the American Natural Hygiene Society that will help you.

As you get more experienced, you'll probably simplify your food preparation quite a bit. After all, the more time you spend playing around in the kitchen, the less time you have to play everywhere else. You'll have more time to enjoy the great outdoors—hiking, canoeing, playing sports, and gardening; and the great indoors—reading great books, writing love poems, painting and drawing, making clothes, and, of course, creating the next generation of Natural Hygienists!

← *Key idea!*

Breakfast ideas

A breakfast made from fresh fruit, lettuce, and celery is a quick, easy, and delicious way to start the day. Be flexible with your fruit choices, based on what is ripe and available in the market. Fruit smoothies (blended fruits) are also fun. Cooked oatmeal with a few raisins is another good breakfast choice that adds variety and some welcome additional calories. Here are a few ideas.

- *Fresh Fruit Salad (such as bananas, apples, and strawberries), lettuce and celery, 1-2 oz. of almonds or sunflower seeds*
- *Orange Juice Smoothie (blend orange, banana, and kiwi), oatmeal with raisins*
- *Melon Salad Supreme (variety of melons and berries), lettuce and celery*
- *Deluxe Citrus Salad (variety of citrus fruit, berries, and kiwi), lettuce and celery, 1 oz. of raw, unsalted almonds or sunflower seeds*

Lunch ideas

Eat a large amount of fresh salad vegetables every day!

Eat a very big fresh vegetable salad every day at lunch. You can include all of your favorite vegetables—lettuce, celery, sweet peppers, broccoli, cauliflower, cucumber, tomato, jicama, carrots, beets, peas, cabbage, and more! You can assemble a different combination each day for variety. Add to this the Tomato Avocado dressing listed below (or better ones that you make up!), and you have the beginings of a feast. In addition to your salad, have a large plate of steamed vegetables, plus a baked potato, or a bowl of soup. Here are some ideas.

- *Large vegetable salad, dressing, steamed vegetables, baked potato*
- *Carrot juice, large vegetable salad, dressing, Potato-Vegetable Soup, brown rice*
- *Corn on the cob, large vegetable salad, dressing, steamed vegetables*
- *Mixed vegetable juice, large vegetable salad, dressing, steamed vegetables, baked potato*
- *Large vegetable salad, dressing, steamed vegetables, steamed quinoa*

Dinner ideas

Dinner also begins with a fresh vegetable salad (or mixed vegetable platter), along with a healthful salad dressing or a little lemon juice. Follow this up with a helping of rice and steamed vegetables, a hearty soup, or a tasty casserole.

Here are some sample dinner ideas.

- *Large vegetable salad, dressing, Brown Rice-Lentil Stew*
- *Mixed vegetable platter, dressing, steamed vegetables, Split Pea-Yam Soup over brown rice*

- *Vegetable salad, dressing, steamed vegetables, baked potatoes*
- *Vegetable salad, dressing, Potato-Vegetable Soup, Brown Rice-Lentil Stew*

Recipes

The following recipes are intended to give you a starting point for making the transition to a healthful diet. Don't be afraid to come up with your own variations!

Delicious transitional recipes to help you get started!

Tomato Avocado Dressing
1/2 tomato, diced; 1 avocado, peeled and sliced
1/2 cup celery juice or water; 8 basil leaves
Place all ingredients in a blender or food processor and puree until smooth. Serve immediately.

Brown Rice-Lentil Stew
4 cups lentils; 6 cups water; 2 cups celery juice
3 carrots, diced; 4 ribs celery, diced
3 tomatoes, diced; 1 red bell pepper, diced
1 sweet potato, peeled and diced
1 bunch spinach; 2 cups brown rice
2 cups water
Bring 2 cups of water to a boil; stir in rice. When the water comes back to a vigorous boil, put lid on pan and turn heat down to a very low setting, approximately 15-20 minutes. In an 8-quart soup pot, bring all the other ingredients to a boil. Reduce the heat to medium-low and simmer for 45 minutes. Mix rice with vegetables to serve.

Potato-Vegetable Soup
3 russet potatoes, peeled
1 large Yukon Gold potato
1 large yam, peeled; 3 ribs celery; 1/4 head cabbage
2 large rutabagas, peeled
10 button mushrooms, washed
Water or soup stock as needed
In a food processor or by hand, slice all of the ingredients and place in an 8-quart soup pot. Cover the vegetables with the

liquid. For added flavor, add 3-4 cups of leftover steamed vegetables, chopped. Bring to a boil, then simmer for 40 minutes, or until all vegetables are tender. Blend in food processor, and serve.

Split Pea–Yam Soup
9 cups soup stock; 2 cups dry split peas
3 large yams and 2 potatoes, peeled and diced
3 ribs celery, diced
1 yellow onion, chopped or 1 Tbsp. dried flakes
1 tsp. dill; 1 Tbsp. garlic powder
1/2 tsp. oregano; 1/2 tsp. thyme; 2 bay leaves

Bring the soup stock or water and peas to a boil while preparing the other ingredients. Add the yams and potatoes and simmer for 30 minutes, stirring occasionally. Add the celery, onion, and spices and simmer until peas are tender (about 30 minutes). Remove the bay leaves. If a smooth texture is desired, blend in a food processor until smooth.

▼ ▼ ▼ ▼ ▼

In the next chapter, learn the latest thinking on the Natural Hygiene practice of food combining.

6

Food Combining Made Easier

The popular practice of food combining—eating simple meals with foods selected based on the concept of digestive compatibility—originated with Natural Hygiene.

Food combining found its greatest proponent in Dr. Herbert Shelton, one of the founders of the American Natural Hygiene Society, who published a little booklet titled *Food Combining Made Easy.* Dr. Shelton's practice as a physician brought him into contact with tens of thousands of people who had developed diseases that were reversible through the practice of Natural Hygiene, including dramatic dietary changes.

Through experience, Dr. Shelton discovered that his patients, especially those with eating disorders such as compulsive overeating, could avoid the dietary excesses that had contributed to their ill health if they were very rigid in their eating habits.

In 1951, when Dr. Shelton first published *Food Combining Made Easy,* much less was known about nutrition and human physiology than is known today. Dr. Shelton hypothesized that indiscriminate combinations of foods, which he classified into categories (proteins, starches, fruits, and vegetables), were indigestible in the human stomach. To help his patients avoid "bad combinations" of foods, he devised a set of food combining rules, which are summarized in the following three recommendations:

1. *Don't eat concentrated proteins and concentrated starches at the same meal.*
2. *Don't eat fruit with either concentrated proteins or concentrated starches.*
3. *Vegetables can be eaten with either concentrated proteins or concentrated starches.*

Can aid in weight loss!

Many people have become acquainted with the concept of food combining from reading about it in the best-selling book, *Fit For Life,* co-authored by Harvey Diamond and Marilyn Diamond. *Fit For Life* helped millions of people transform their eating habits, and many were delightfully surprised to find that, when they simplified their meals, they lost weight.

The real benefits of food combining

Although there is no scientific evidence to back up the assertion that we must eat only certain combinations of foods at a single meal or face dire consequences, everyone who has successfully employed food combining has enjoyed some very real benefits—they eat simpler meals, and are much less likely to overeat. The indigestion and other problems experienced when foods are "improperly combined" are more likely related to overeating (especially overeating on concentrated foods) and/or the digestive limitations of the person involved than anything that can reasonably be attributed to "bad combinations."

Most of us developed atrocious eating habits in early life and need to make dramatic changes if we want to be healthy. Food combining offers us a new pattern of eating, one that helps us make the transition to a healthful, plant-based diet, and helps us develop a new and healthier attitude toward eating.

← A new pattern of eating!

Natural Hygiene diet

Research resoundingly supports the two central dietary recommendations of Natural Hygiene—eat a plant-based diet, and do not overeat. In addition, there are further

"Every day you should eat something from each of the five basic food groups: fried blubber, boiled blubber, stewed blubber, baked blubber, and raw blubber."

benefits because a large portion of the Natural Hygiene diet is uncooked, and because the emphasis is on vegetables, rather than grains, in contrast to other vegetarian diets. When these recommendations are adopted, food combining offers little, if any, additional benefit.

But for those people who are not yet willing or able to adopt the Natural Hygiene dietary recommendations, food combining may make a significant difference. Dr. Shelton targeted *Food Combining Made Easy* to just such an audience. He recognized that if people were going to eat meat, fish, poultry, eggs, and dairy products,

"You may not believe it, but it's made from a mix."

they would be less likely to overeat if they were limited to just one of these "foods" at a meal. That way, they would not be eating as much concentrated food.

Dr. Shelton realized that it would help people even more if they avoided other concentrated foods, such as complex carbohydrates, when eating animal products. To a certain degree, food combining was an attempt to minimize the price people had to pay for eating foods that they should not have been eating in the first place.

Feeding children

Food combining rules can be overrestrictive for children. Many growing children are picky eaters. Arbitrarily restricting foods that they are eating can lead to problems. The International Association of Hygienic Physicians (IAHP) is a group of doctors who utilize the principles of Natural Hygiene in their practices. (See Chapter 15.) These physicians see many children whose well-meaning parents are trying to put food combining above the primary Hygienic food recommendation—to eat a wide variety of whole, natural, plant foods.

Eating a plant-based diet, and not overeating, are much more important than food combining!

These physicians feel that it is wrong for parents to overemphasize food combining. Children are very peer-oriented. It is hard enough for them to forego the junk food—burgers, soft drinks, pizza, candy, ice cream, etc.— their friends eat, without having to worry about food combining. Parents should be happy if their children are willing to eat whole, natural foods.

Natural Hygiene: the science of health

People with digestive problems can benefit by simplifying their meals. But food combining as a general admonition to the overall population is not supported by either science or experience. Food combining is not a necessity for people who are eating healthful, plant-based diets. However, food combining can help curtail appetite. This may help people avoid overeating and help them keep their weight down.

> **The benefits of Natural Hygiene are not linked to food combining.**

The American Natural Hygiene Society and the IAHP still recommend that people eat simple, uncomplicated meals. Neither group is asking anyone to stop practicing food combining if it is helping them to live more healthfully. But both groups think that it is time for Natural Hygienists to focus less on food combining, because it creates unnecessary stress for people. In addition, opponents of Natural Hygiene have used food combining as evidence that Natural Hygiene is not based on science.

▼ ▼ ▼ ▼ ▼

In the next chapter, you will learn about the vital importance of rest and sleep.

▼ ▼ ▼ ▼ ▼ ▼ ▼ ▼ ▼

7

Sleep and Your Health

Energy is the key to health. Nothing can replace what sleep gives us in the way of energy and healing. One way of describing health is in terms of the degree of functional efficiency of the cells that make up your tissues, organs, organ systems, and all other parts of your body. The functional efficiency of your cells depends both upon the caloric energy that comes from food, and the electrical energy that comes from sleep.

There are different stages of sleep, and we go through them in cycles. A cycle lasts about 90 minutes. We start with stage one, which is very light, then stage two, which is a little deeper, and then stage three, which is associated with delta wave brain activity (the slowest, most relaxed brain wave activity). Stage four sleep is our deepest stage of sleep. We spend anywhere from 20-45 minutes in stage four sleep. Then we gradually come back through stage three, stage two, and stage one. Then we have an episode of rapid eye movement (REM) sleep, where even though our eyes are closed, they are mov-

◂ *Deep sleep is vital to health.*

ing under our eyelids.

Sleep deprivation can lead to serious problems.

A deficiency of stage four sleep causes problems. Studies have shown that when otherwise healthy people are deprived of delta sleep for a few days, fibromyalgia (a condition of generalized tender spots of the body associated with fatigue) sets in. Once these people are allowed to get their usual amount of delta sleep for a few days, the fibromyalgia goes away.

Sleep and healing

At the deepest levels of sleep, the body releases its most important healing hormones, including growth hormone and testosterone. The release of these hormones is inhibited during stages one and two sleep, and when you are awake.

Sleep enables you to recover from your everyday

*"No, I'm afraid you **cannot** claim an energy depletion allowance."*

wear and tear and to heal. Without adequate sleep, you accumulate all the wear and tear until you get sick.

When you do not get enough sleep, you have a lower energy level. When your energy is low, nothing functions normally. For example, your immune system will not function as well, and you will be more prone to infections. Cognitive function (brain function) and emotional function are impaired as well.

When you are tired, you don't have the energy to cope with things that go wrong. You may become angry more easily. If low energy persists long enough, permanent damages can occur.

Chronic fatigue syndrome

The symptoms of chronic fatigue syndrome are decreased immune function, decreased cognitive function, decreased emotional function, and decreased bodily functions (digestive, etc.). People who suffer from this affliction are often highly motivated, intelligent, responsible, and tend to be geared toward perfectionism. They often have long-standing sleep problems. They have depleted their energy by taking on so many responsibilities. They frequently have difficulty recharging their batteries because of poor sleep habits. People in this situation often need additional hours of sleep every day, for a considerable length of time, for them to recover.

Sleep is critical to recovery!

An exhausting cycle

Pushing yourself—whether by emotional, physical, mental, or chemical stimulation—causes the release of adrenaline. The more tired you get and the more you push yourself, the more adrenaline you cause to be released.

As a result, you may have a problem winding down at the end of the day and getting to sleep.

The adrenaline interferes with your ability to sleep, and lack of deep sleep inhibits the release of the healing hormones. As a result, you wake up tired the next day. But because you have to get through another day, you push yourself even harder, causing the release of even more adrenaline.

The way to stop this cycle is to stop pushing yourself. If you wake up in the morning and you are too tired to function, you should spend the day catching up on your sleep—even if it means staying home from work. Learning to listen to your body will help you stay healthier. A few missed days from work to prevent serious illness will mean fewer missed days in the long run.

Sleep not a luxury

Key idea! ➡ Taking care of yourself is not a luxury; it is a responsibility! Getting enough sleep is part of that responsibility. You need to recover from everyday wear and tear so that you have the energy to function and to live life the way you know it can be lived.

▼ ▼ ▼ ▼ ▼

In the next chapter, you will learn the importance of exercise in a healthful lifestyle.

8

The Benefits of Exercise

Natural Hygiene emphasizes the importance of exercise as part of a total healthful lifestyle. Exercise, rest, and sleep are major components in lifelong health. A regular, well thought-out exercise program will help ensure that you maintain strength and flexibility throughout your life and, more importantly, will provide many lasting health benefits.

Exercise is an important component of lifelong health!

Whenever you do anything that is physically vigorous and active, it causes your body to adapt—by building stronger muscles, stronger bones, and a stronger heart.

Most people tend to be less physically active as they get older, so a gradual decline in fitness is very typical. As a result, when they encounter an unexpected challenge or emergency—such as an accident or any severe emotional stress—they are far less able to cope with, and survive, the situation.

Natural Hygiene urges everyone to engage in an exercise program designed with their individual goals and capacities in mind. From a Natural Hygiene point of view, you need not think in terms of running marathon races or attempting to match the physiques of professional bodybuilders. The goal of exercise is to enhance your health, fitness, and joy of life.

The beneficial effects of exercise

A strong heart and circulatory system!

One of the top benefits of exercise is a strong heart and circulatory system. A well-conditioned heart can pump more blood with fewer beats. It is more efficient. It also grows more blood vessels to carry oxygen and nutrients to its walls, to its pump. Blood pressure is lower. Blood does not clot as easily, so heart attack risk goes down. Cholesterol levels go down. The HDL (high density lipoprotein)—the "good" part of the cholesterol level—goes up, and the LDL (low density lipoprotein)—the "bad" part—tends to go down. Exercise even appears to be able to postpone the aging process in the heart. So-called "normal changes of aging" may just be the result of a sedentary lifestyle.

Another beneficial effect of an active lifestyle is better regulation of your metabolic functions, such as control of blood sugar level and metabolic rate. Exercise lowers the blood sugar level and increases the body's sensitivity or ability to use insulin. Both of these factors are very important to a condition called adult-onset diabetes, which tends to affect people as they become older. It is a disease characterized by high blood sugar levels, and if these levels get too high, people are typically advised to take insulin in order to control them.

The good news is that exercise combined with a proper diet can help diabetics lower or eliminate the need for this artificial insulin. By increasing the body's

"You know—things like jogger's knee, low back pain, hypoglycemia..."

sensitivity to insulin, the *amount* of insulin the body produces, even though it may be low, will often be enough to control their blood sugar.

Stronger muscles and bones

Another benefit of a good exercise program is the strengthening of muscle and, even more importantly, bone that results from exercising regularly. Strong muscles help protect joints and enable you to do more work with less fatigue. Strong bones are less likely to break with an accidental fall or other injury.

Helps prevent osteoporosis

This is important for women because they are more susceptible to a disease process called osteoporosis, especially as they age. Osteoporosis is due to loss of calcium from bones. It is very common in the U.S., and it causes a lot of pain and suffering in the elderly. A combination of an Hygienic diet and regular weight-bearing exercise is essential in preventing this debilitating condition.

Physically fit bodies have better functioning immune systems, and physically fit people have more success combating anxiety, depression, and stress. These two factors are related because stress is known to decrease immune function, and exercise is known to combat stress. It may be that the stress-fighting ability of exercise is what makes it an immune-enhancing activity.

Important for weight management

Exercise also is important in weight management. Firm, toned muscles have a more pleasing appearance, and exercise helps us form the enzymes that burn fat rather than store it. Exercise also improves the quality of sleep.

Exercise can help you keep your weight down!

An interesting study was done that illustrates the relationship between diet, exercise, and weight loss.

A large group of women was divided into three groups. The first group was given 500 fewer calories per day than usual; the second group was given 250 fewer calories per day than usual *and* was required to do 250 calories worth of exercise each day. The third group ate their normal amount of calories, but were required to do 500 calories worth of exercise each day.

At the end of 16 weeks, researchers found (as you would expect) that all of the women lost weight. But the women in the first group, who only reduced their calories, lost a lot of muscle tissue. The third group, who only did the exercise, increased their muscle mass and lost weight, too, but not as much as the women in the first group. The second group, the combination group, did the best. They lost the most body weight, lost the most body fat, and increased their muscle mass.

Importance of rest and sleep

If your goal is to reach your optimum level of health, physical activity is extremely important, but it must be kept in balance with the other health-promoting factors, particularly rest and sleep. Healing and body repair occur mostly during sleep. The anabolic hormones, the hormones that promote repair of muscle tissue and other tissue, are released during sleep.

← Key idea!

If you are not sleeping properly, you can't initiate that healing process. The proper amount of sleep varies with your state of health, your level of stress, and your degree of fitness. Many factors are involved.

Rest other than sleep also is important, especially as you get older. You must allow recovery time between bouts of vigorous exercise, or else alternate the types of activities that you do to allow the different sets of muscles time to repair themselves between sessions.

Designing a program that's right for you

Since every individual is different, exercise programs should be tailored to meet individual needs. The cornerstone of most programs will be aerobic exercise, but some people may need to focus on other exercises, such as strength training, weight lifting, or stretching.

Aerobic means the exercise is steady and non-stop and lasts a minimum of 12 minutes. That means 12 minutes at the level you are trying to reach. Aerobic exercise needs to raise your heart rate into the range between

65% and 80% of your maximum heart rate, depending upon your age and your physical fitness. It should be done a minimum of four times a week to achieve beneficial results.

Start with an activity that you enjoy. Walking, jogging, running, cycling, rowing, cross-country skiing, dancing, jumping rope, and climbing stairs are all non-stop, rhythmic activities that you can do for at least 12 minutes that will get your heart rate up and keep it there.

To find your training rate, subtract your age from 220 and then take 60 percent and 80 percent of this number. This is the target range for your pulse. At the halfway point and at the end of your routine, take your pulse for six seconds and add a zero to the number. Before very long you will recognize your aerobic training intensity without continually taking your pulse.

People who are on medications, who are older, who have not been active for a long time, or who have a condition that might warrant it, should consult their doctor and make it their business to research how their condition impacts their ability to start an exercise program.

Get started today

You are extraordinarily capable of transforming yourself at any age. Your daily habits, your mental attitudes, and your expectations for yourself play a major role in what you will achieve in your life. Get involved in regular aerobic activity, and experience the joy of being fit!

▼ ▼ ▼ ▼ ▼

In the next chapter, you will learn how to create a healthful environment for yourself!

▼ ▼ ▼ ▼ ▼ ▼ ▼ ▼ ▼

9

Creating Your Healthful Environment

We face tremendous threats to the quality of our air, water, and soil. We must take a stand against this rampant destruction, both by modifying our own behavior and by voting with our dollars—supporting businesses and organizations that do right by Mother Earth, and shunning those that don't.

← Stick up for your Mother!

While we may feel powerless—as individuals—to stop nuclear radioactivity, oil spills, war, and clear-cutting of forests, we can take steps to improve all of the local environmental factors that are *within* our control.

To be healthy, we need to conscientiously secure for ourselves pure food, clean air and water, adequate sunshine, and freedom from as much pollution (indoor and outdoor) as possible, including noise.

Insist on the best for yourself and your loved ones!

The impact of all the environmental insults we face in modern life is a subject all of its own and is beyond the scope of this handbook. However, certain general recommendations can be made, and we all can support local and national efforts to protect the environment.

Fresh air

Clean, fresh air is vital for optimal health. Take steps to help improve the quality of the air you breathe. Change the air filters in your home air conditioning and heating systems on a regular basis. Air filters are available that will enable you to further control the quality of air that you breathe indoors. Stale air can be removed by opening your windows regularly to "air" your house out.

Walk more, drive less. Carpool whenever possible. Keep your automobile in clean, efficient running order. Spend time outside in areas away from traffic or during those times when traffic is at a minimum.

Plant more trees! Plant trees! Trees help clean the air by filtering dust and pollution, and they also convert carbon dioxide into life-giving oxygen. If your home or your workplace is in an intolerably polluted area, seriously consider moving.

How much sunshine?

Exposure to sunlight is vital to vitamin D production! Natural Hygienists have always advocated plenty of fresh air and sunshine. The most well-known beneficial effect of skin exposure to sunlight is the production of vitamin D. Vitamin D is needed for the body to absorb dietary calcium. Some scientists think that bone loss in the elderly may be partly related to a vitamin D deficiency from lack of exposure to sufficient sunlight.

Exposure to sunlight is essential for human health. But we need to avoid the damaging effects of *overexposure* to sunlight and ultraviolet radiation, especially now that the ozone layer has been damaged. Too much sun exposure can cause premature aging of the skin and the danger of skin cancer. Enjoy your time in the sun in the morning or late in the afternoon.

"I thought he would run all sorts of scientific tests."

Pure water

Natural Hygienists recommend that you drink the purest water available—which is usually distilled water. If no distilled water is available, get the next best available—which is usually water purified by reverse osmosis.

Always drink the purest water available.

Since most water is contaminated with minerals, heavy metals, other elements, chemical compounds, and organic materials (many of which are toxic), it is wise to drink the purest water you can get.

It is sometimes claimed that distilled water "leaches" nutrients. Water does not have the ability to leach nutrients. The body carefully controls its nutrient balance with an array of hormonal and biologic controls. Claims that distilled water is "dead" or can "leach" minerals have no scientific support. By the same token, Natural Hygienists do not attempt to bestow any special virtues on distilled water; it is simply the purest water obtainable by the general public.

Noise pollution

We all are being exposed to an increasingly noisy environment—from the sounds of jet planes overhead to traffic in the streets. You may not be able to control *all* of the sounds that enter into your environment, but you can help to minimize their intrusion in several ways.

Take steps to minimize the noise pollution in your life!

Trees and shrubbery can help muffle the outdoor sounds of traffic and loud machinery. Plant them wherever practical. Trees improve the quality of the air, provide shade in the summer (helping to reduce cooling bills), and help beautify your immediate environment.

Sometimes family members want to play their TVs, radios, computer games, and other electronic equipment very loudly. Try to persuade them to keep the noise level down. If all else fails, invest in a good pair of ear plugs. These can help to reduce your noise intake in situations you cannot control, especially if you have to be around loud machinery, noisy computer printers, or other loud environments. If you work at home, set up your working space in a quiet part of the house.

The important thing is to create as healthful an environment as possible to complement your healthful diet and lifestyle.

▼ ▼ ▼ ▼ ▼

Next you will learn how to live sanely in a pretty insane world!

▼ ▼ ▼ ▼ ▼ ▼ ▼ ▼ ▼

10

Being Different With Style

Natural Hygiene can be described in precise, scientific terms. It can be measured, tested, evaluated, and written down like so many rules and regulations. It is also a beautiful and remarkable system. Its message is clear and pure, simple and direct, and easy to understand.

But unless Natural Hygiene is put into practice, it is lifeless, dead on a page of some forgotten book on a dusty shelf. No book or tape or lecture can bring Natural Hygiene to life. We give it the only life it can ever have—when we put it into practice.

Portrait of a Natural Hygienist

What happens when we put Natural Hygiene into practice? Health happens! Our eyes shine. Our bodies grow stronger. Our minds become clearer.

← Health is normal and natural!

Natural Hygienists share the goals of people everywhere. We want health, happiness, peace, and prosperity for ourselves, our families, friends and neighbors—

those nearby and those around the world.

We appreciate beauty and harmony. We respect life and freedom. We want to live in a world that is comforting, nurturing, and protective of us. We want to feel a part of our community. We want to live interesting, wholesome, and productive lives.

We want to love and be loved. We want to see our children and grandchildren grow and flourish in a clean, healthy environment, safe from war, poverty, pollution, crime, and exploitation.

Living sanely in an insane world

Going along with this crowd could be deadly! ➡ Unfortunately, we live in a world gone mad. If things were the way they should be, our customs and traditions, laws, government agencies, and educational institutions would lead us all to full, rich, healthy, and happy lives. Our parents and teachers would teach us how to live and how to become fully functioning human beings. Our surrounding environment would be supportive of healthy, wholesome living.

In this ideal setting we could live just like our families and friends and everybody else because it would make sense. We could go along with the crowd because the crowd would be on the right track.

But we don't live in an ideal world. We live in a world where the traditions, folklore, culture, and customs lead not to the beautiful life we all want, but to great and frequent pain, suffering, and sorrow for so many people.

Different with good reason

In the world we live in, we cannot go along with the crowd. We have to do the things that actually lead to the good life. And what actually leads to it is very different from what we were brought up to think.

True, we cannot say with absolute certainty that Natural Hygiene is the ultimate lifestyle. But until we are convinced that there is something even better, doesn't it make sense to live the best way we know how?

Ambassadors for health

Not everyone is going to instantly join us on the road to health. We can share our ideas with loved ones and friends; we can show the world by good example how much we are enjoying the trip. But in the end, we must walk that road whether anyone else walks with us or not. And we can walk with confidence, knowing that through constant investigation and attention we give ourselves our best chance of reaching our destination.

Let's face it. Living as a Natural Hygienist makes you different, a very special kind of different. You are ahead of your time, and you stand out because of the high quality lifestyle choices you make. As a result, you are also going to attract attention. How you handle that attention will have a profound effect on your life and the lives of those around you.

Talking the walk

In some ways, it is harder to talk effectively about Natural Hygiene than it is to live it. Doing it is easy. Trying to explain it to other people can be a challenge. Fortunately, while there is no "right" way to talk about it, there

"No more, thanks. I've had my minimum daily requirement of DDT."

are some tried and true strategies that work.

Until you are knowledgeable and experienced in your new lifestyle, don't talk about it too much. First, learn as much as you can about your subject. Then put what you have learned into practice.

If you are new to Natural Hygiene and the occasion calls for you to say something about it, keep your comments short, simple, and honest. Say you are "trying it," or that you are "experimenting."

If you were to ask someone why they were eating an ice cream sundae, they most likely would say, "I like it," or, "It tastes so good." These can be the same answers you give when you are asked about your favorite foods. You don't have to be a walking encyclopedia of nutritional expertise.

Keep it simple!

You wouldn't expect to become an overnight expert in car repair, carpentry, or chemistry. Don't make the mistake of trying to become an instant expert on fasting, nutrition, and physiology simply by reading a book.

A shining example

Carry yourself with poise and dignity. Once you have mastered the basics of Natural Hygiene, you automatically become a type of leader, one who has achieved proficiency in the art of living. Carry yourself like a leader. Be kind, respectful, positive, patient, and a good and thoughtful listener.

People will be attracted to you. Treat them the way you would like to be treated—with kindness and compassion. Emphasize the things you have in common with them, not your differences.

You are now a style setter. You don't need to be thinking about "fitting in" or going along with the crowd. You are a leader, not a follower. You don't have to wonder "what people will think." Can you imagine Einstein and Gandhi worrying about "fitting in"? How about Eleanor Roosevelt or Rachel Carson? They were leaders. They followed their hearts and minds, not convention.

Natural Hygiene makes you a style setter!

Can you imagine Elizabeth Taylor worrying whether or not to wear her big diamond pendant when she goes out? Do you think she worries about "fitting in"? No. She is a style setter. So are you.

The best approach to Natural Hygiene is to become knowledgeable and experienced, to become a picture of health and happiness, and to teach by your good cheer and good example that you have found a wonderfully satisfying way of life.

Food for thought

When you find yourself in situations where your food choices will be under discussion, there are two basic ways you can respond—gracefully or defensively. The American Natural Hygiene Society recommends that you respond gracefully.

Key idea! ➡

When questioned about your diet, you can charmingly change the subject, or express your very well-seasoned views in a delightful, informative way. Your choice!

The easiest way to change the subject is to ask questions about topics that interest the people you are with. Most people would rather talk about themselves than listen to you anyway. If someone is particularly persistent in cross-examining you, excuse yourself with a smile and go to another room.

Knowing what to say and when to say it is the first

"Stop the presses. They're veggies!"

step in good communication. Thanksgiving dinner is not the time to lecture your relatives about their eating and drinking habits.

If you are inclined to talk about your new diet, speak in an interesting way that will attract listeners. If you are not successful at capturing your listener's attention, you have wasted all the work that went into discovering what to say in the first place. Be upbeat and positive!

World renowned advertising executive Bill Bernbach, who knew as much about effective communication as anybody, had this to say:

> *"The truth isn't the truth until people believe you; and they can't believe you if they don't know what you're saying; and they can't know what you're saying if they don't listen to you; and they won't listen to you if you're not interesting. And you won't be interesting unless you say things freshly, originally, imaginatively."*

Here are some tips guaranteed to help you win (and keep) friends while you are influencing them.

1. *Be yourself.* The only person you have to convince is you. You have a right to experiment. And you don't have to convince anybody else to try it.
2. *Be honest.* If people ask questions you can't answer, don't be afraid to say, "I don't know." You don't have to pretend to know more than you do.
3. *Don't make trouble.* You don't have to give a lecture every time you go out to dinner. If no one asks you about your new habits, don't bring them up. If they do, don't be afraid to change the subject.
4. *Pick your spots.* Timing is important. Before embarking on a long lecture to friends, be sure that they have both a genuine interest and the time to listen.
5. *Know your subject.* It never hurts to know what you are talking about. Natural Hygiene is not an easy subject to learn (or to explain in five minutes). Avoid the tendency to talk too much about something you've just heard or read about. Read, think, test, and evaluate before you make your opinions public.

▼ ▼ ▼ ▼ ▼

In the next chapter, you will learn about the role that fasting can play in a healthful lifestyle.

11

The Benefits of Fasting

Fasting plays an important role in Natural Hygiene. When properly utilized, fasting is a safe and effective means of maximizing the body's self-healing capacities. The benefits that can be derived from a properly conducted fast can be truly amazing. In fact, fasting is such a powerful therapeutic tool that Hygienic physicians make it a primary component of their primary-care education and their postgraduate study. (The International Association of Hygienic Physicians offers a certification program in fasting supervision for qualified doctors. See Chapter 15.)

Before describing some of the many advantages of fasting, let's define it. *Fasting is the complete abstinence from all substances except pure water, in an environment of total rest.*

◂ Fasting should be thought of as resting.

It is important to keep in mind that fasting is only one part of the *total* health-supporting program we call Natural Hygiene. Health results from healthful living. No matter how successful a fasting experience might be, it needs to be followed by a consistently healthful lifestyle. You need to provide yourself with the requirements of health—especially in the areas of diet, environment, activity, and psychology.

Learn to respect your body's needs.

One aspect of Natural Hygiene is the recognition of the importance of "listening" to your body, and respecting what it has to "say." Fasting can be as simple as skipping a meal or a few meals during a period of time when you are not hungry—like when you don't feel good. Natural Hygiene takes the position that your body's needs should be respected. When your body tells you that it is hungry—*eat;* when it tells you it is tired—*rest or sleep;* when it is cold—*seek warmth.* In this light, fasting can be seen as nothing more than an intelligent attempt to honor your individual physiological needs.

History of fasting in Natural Hygiene

Throughout history, people have noticed that when they become acutely ill, they lose their appetites. The early Hygienic physicians reasoned that there must be some physiological reason for this loss of appetite. Through observation and experimentation, they discovered that fasting (as defined above) allows the body to make a unique physiological adaptation. In the fasting state, the duration and intensity of the symptoms of illness, such as inflammation, mucus production, fever, diarrhea, etc. are often dramatically reduced. In fact, fasting has been found to be the most efficient and powerful means available to facilitate *self-healing*.

Fasting often relieves symptoms.

Further experimentation and observation found that fasting is also effective in the resolution of chronic disease. Chronic disease—including heart disease, diabetes, cancer, arthritis, respiratory illness, autoimmune disease, etc.—can be the result of several different factors. These factors can include things we can learn to control—inappropriate diet, such as the consumption of animal products and refined foods; the use of drugs, including tobacco, alcohol, coffee, etc.; a lack of adequate sleep or exercise; excess psychological stress—and factors that are more difficult or even impossible to control—exposure to environmental stressors, such as pollution, radiation, excess noise, etc.; and hereditary factors.

Fasting can be an important tool to help resolve the symptoms of both acute illness and chronic disease, but its benefits are not limited to dealing with symptoms.

◄ Resolving chronic disease

Fasting can help you make the transition to healthful living, which will allow your body to heal itself to the greatest degree possible and help prevent acute and chronic illness from recurring in the future.

Who can benefit from a fast?

It is difficult to break the habits and patterns of behavior we have established over many years. The typical Western lifestyle leads to taste buds acclimated to stimulating foods, muscles that are flabby, and a nervous system that depends on stimulatory drugs (such as caffeine) to keep it going despite a lack of sleep. Sometimes, when first attempting to improve their diets and lifestyles, people find healthful food unappetizing, exercise painful, and the symptoms of withdrawal from stimulants unbearable. The slow process of detoxification that accompanies the cessation of bad habits can cause unpleasant symptoms to persist for weeks or months.

Jump ➡ start your new health program!

Fasting is a method of speeding up the detoxification process. It can be an intense and sometimes unpleasant experience, but it is highly effective. After fasting, healthful foods often taste delicious, and pernicious habits often have much less appeal. Fasting is the most efficient means available to overcome dependencies on a variety of drugs, including caffeine, nicotine, alcohol, marijuana, and others. Educational programs available at Hygienic institutions specializing in fasting supervision help people to develop the skills necessary to select and prepare healthful foods, develop a sensible exercise program, and find emotional support.

Some individuals appear and feel healthy, but still manifest abnormal signs such as high blood pressure,

"Coming to bat is Garrison, the shortstop. He's hitting .274, with 5 homers, his blood sugar and cholesterol are normal, and we're waiting for the results of his drug and alcohol tests."

elevated blood levels of cholesterol, triglycerides, glucose, uric acid or liver enzyme imbalances, etc. Fasting often can help restore higher levels of health and vitality and eliminate these signs that are associated with disease. Fasting also can be used as a diagnostic tool in uncovering subclinical pathology that may exist.

Fasting may offer its greatest potential in the prevention of disease. A person may have adopted a health promoting diet and lifestyle to overcome disease, and be completely free of all signs and symptoms of disease. But he or she may choose to use fasting as a preventive

Fasting can be an important aid in prevention.

measure to allow the body to eliminate the metabolic products that might otherwise accumulate (within the cells of the body) despite their best efforts.

Whether fasting is used in the transition to a healthful diet and lifestyle, to overcome the signs and symptoms of disease, or as a preventive measure, it is a powerful tool for helping sick people get well and healthy people to stay healthy.

Fasting also can be a powerful tool in efforts to reverse serious illness. Conditions that respond favorably to fasting and aggressive diet and lifestyle changes include headache, hypoglycemia, rheumatoid arthritis, asthma, heart disease, high blood pressure, diabetes, colitis, psoriasis, lupus, and uterine fibroids.

Contraindication to fasting

Not every individual is a candidate for fasting. In some instances, a person's medical condition will preclude the undertaking of a therapeutic fast. Hygienic physicians will consider a number of factors before recommending a fast. They review the patient's medical history; perform a comprehensive physical examination, including appropriate laboratory or specialized diagnostic tests; and review the findings with the patient. Recommendations might include dietary and lifestyle changes, exercise programs, and—when indicated—fasting at an appropriate institution.

Not every individual or every condition will respond to fasting and conservative treatment. Occasionally, medical care may be necessary. When a medical consultation or treatment is indicated, the safest methods available should be utilized.

The best place to fast

With the possible exception of very short fasts in response to loss of appetite due to acute disease—such as a cold, or fever—all fasting should be undertaken in an Hygienic institution under the direct supervision of a physician trained and certified in fasting supervision.

Fasting in a Natural Hygiene institution offers several advantages. The most important is the constant availability of an experienced doctor to guide and advise you. Most institutions have an educational program designed to help you better understand Natural Hygiene—the science of health. The benefits of being in a clean, quiet, and emotionally supportive environment should not be underestimated. In addition, a timely and proper termination of each fast is critical to the long-term success of the patient. Fasting under the supervision of a trained, qualified doctor is your best assurance of a well-conducted, beneficial fasting experience.

Commonly asked questions about fasting

When is the best time to fast?
The ideal time to fast is when we receive the natural signs from the body to do so. A good example is the loss of appetite that occurs when we develop an acute illness, especially when it is accompanied by fever, chills, or fatigue. These are the times when we will secure the greatest benefits from fasting. Our body is telling us to stop eating, keep warm, and rest until we feel better.

Unfortunately, family, community, and economic situations often exist that prevent, or at least deter, people from fasting at those times. Consequently, some people simply choose to fast for longer periods on their vacations. Many people who suffer with chronic illness have long passed the acute stages of disease when the body signaled them to fast. They need to set aside an arbitrary period of time to fast.

Is fasting one day a week recommended?
On the surface, fasting one day a week seems like a good way to recover from the stresses of the previous six days. But if you adopt a proper lifestyle, that includes adequate rest, appropriate diet, stress management, and exercise, there will be no need to arbitrarily set aside one day each week to recover from your indiscretions.

BENEFITS OF FASTING ▼ 97

Ideally, a fast day is a rest day. If you can't find time to rest during the week, it is unlikely that you will find the time for a full day of bed rest on the weekend. And what happens if, on the day you have chosen to fast, you awake with a roaring appetite? Should you suppress the natural signals to eat?

Is fasting a good way to lose weight?
It may be acceptable to begin a new lifestyle with a fast to lose weight—as long as the fast is broken properly, and you follow the fast with a proper program of diet and exercise. Fasting to lose weight without making any

"Think back—were there any musicians in the room when we operated on him?"

lifestyle changes is worse than a waste of time. Without the lifestyle changes, you will quickly regain the weight lost during the fast in the form of fat.

To fast or not to fast

The most important advice about fasting is: *Do it right or don't do it.* Complete rest, a supportive environment, and professional supervision is required to ensure that fasting will be a safe and effective experience.

▼ ▼ ▼ ▼ ▼

In the next chapter, you will get answers to the most commonly asked questions about Natural Hygiene.

12

Frequently Asked Questions

Beginning a new health program can be like stepping into new territory. Even though you know the destination is well worth the effort, you may have questions as you set out on your journey.

The following are some of the most frequently asked questions by people who are attempting to make healthful changes in their diets and lifestyles.

Is the Natural Hygiene diet an all-raw food diet?

No. There is no one diet that can meet all people's needs at all times. The American Natural Hygiene Society recommends that people eat a diet derived exclusively from whole, natural foods—fresh fruits and vegetables, whole grains, nuts, and legumes—matched to their individual needs and capabilities.

← Each of us has individual needs!

A diet that might be appropriate for an 80-pound, 80-year-old female may be substantially different from the diet for an active, 220-pound, 20-year-old male athlete. People who have colitis have limited digestive abilities. An older person who has no teeth will need to eat differently from a young growing child.

Our allegiance must be to our individual needs, not to any philosophical or ideological concepts. Our needs can change over time, depending on our activity level, state of health, and the specific goals we are trying to accomplish.

The best diet you can have! ➡

The best diet is the one that enables us to meet our individual energy and nutrient needs, with the least amount of toxic load, or other negative effects, possible. For most people, that translates to a diet made up of a large volume of fresh, raw fruits and vegetables (which are the best source of vitamins, minerals, proteins, fat, water, and fiber); and enough concentrated foods (such as grains, potatoes, yams, legumes, and small quantities of raw, unsalted nuts) to meet our energy needs.

Will I get enough protein on a vegetarian diet?

Getting enough protein should not be a problem! ➡

Yes. A calorie-sufficient diet that includes a broad base of fresh fruits, vegetables (especially leafy greens, yellow vegetables, and cruciferous vegetables), a small amount of seeds and nuts, and complex starches (including potatoes, grains, and legumes) will provide the appropriate amounts of needed nutrients.

As a general guideline, a nutritional program that contains 10-15% total calories from unsaturated nut, seed, and plant-based fats and 10-15% protein (eliminating all animal and dairy products) is recommended.

Will I need to take vitamin and mineral supplements?

No. When you eat a calorie-sufficient diet derived exclusively from whole natural foods—fresh fruits and vegetables, and the variable addition of whole grains, nuts, and legumes—you get an abundant supply of both the *quantity* and *quality* of vitamins your body needs. Vitamin B$_{12}$ is a possible exception.

Vitamins are essential substances needed by the body to catalyze a variety of enzymatic and other functions. If an individual does not obtain the required quantities of these nutrients, health may suffer. If the diet does not provide optimum levels, supplementation may provide some benefits, along with potential risks. If the diet provides the nutrients, supplementation may, in some circumstances, be harmful.

Will I get enough calcium on a Natural Hygiene diet to prevent osteoporosis?
Every natural plant food contains calcium. Vegetarian populations, even those with low calcium intake, have

"What you have isn't serious, but it isn't humorous, either. It's somewhere in-between."

much lower rates of osteoporosis than older women in high meat-eating countries.

The best prevention for osteoporosis is a low-protein diet with an abundance of fresh fruits and vegetables, especially green leafy vegetables, coupled with weight-bearing exercise.

How can I be assured of getting adequate vitamin B_{12} on a vegan (total vegetarian) diet?

Vitamin B_{12} exists in highest concentration in animal and dairy products. However, vitamin B_{12} also is synthesized by bacteria that live on the surface of various vegetables and leafy greens. It also can be found in sea vegetables and some yeast products.

Vitamin B_{12} plays an important role in the production of red blood cells and the integrity of the spinal cord. Although people on a vegan Hygienic diet will often have lower blood levels of B_{12} than people on a

"Hi—sit down—have some vitamins."

conventional meat and dairy diet, the lower levels apparently are sufficient to maintain red cell production and spinal cord health.

If you have been a vegan for more than three to five years, you should take a blood test once a year to evaluate your B_{12} level. Occasionally, people may develop a deficiency. Supplementation may be warranted. If your serum levels drop abnormally low, symptoms of neurological damage can occur and may be permanent.

I want to make effective, long-lasting changes in my lifestyle. But I don't know how to start.
Major change is not something that happens overnight. The process is similar to learning any skillful act. You need to practice it, and to try to be as consistent as possible in your efforts.

Developing new habits takes time!

Over time, as your new practices and behaviors become etched into your nervous system, they will become as strongly ingrained as the old habits. As a practical matter, you may need to make a commitment to avoid some things for a certain period of time. If you have a problem with alcohol, you probably should not take a job as a bartender. If you are trying to get away from sugar, meat, or some other aspect of your diet, avoid situations where you would be tempted to indulge in habits you are trying to break.

Don't be too hard on yourself. Change takes time, patience, self-love, and self-care. It may take years before your new behavior becomes deeply integrated into your life, and becomes a major part of your awareness—your thought processes, your speaking patterns, and so forth. But once you have a breakthrough, and your new behavior becomes a part of you, it is yours forever and no one can take it away from you. Powerful, beneficial results like this are well worth the effort.

Why is it recommended that people take supervised fasts, rather than fasting on their own?

The natural indication to fast is when you lose your appetite, as in the case of acute illness. Usually, under those conditions, the problem resolves and the appetite returns within one to three days. This return of appetite is the body's natural signal to break the fast.

For most people without other health problems, and who are not on any medications, a fast such as the one described above can be conducted naturally on their own. However, in the case of an individual starting a fast *with* an appetite, on an arbitrary date, in order to resolve some chronic condition, it is not a natural indication. Under these circumstances, the indication to fast is for therapeutic reasons, and thus should be conducted under the supervision of a physician trained in fasting supervision.

Most of the time, the supervising physician answers questions, offers support, and monitors the process without intervening. Occasionally, however, his or her experience can prevent unnecessary suffering or disaster.

Fasting with an Hygienic physician certified in fasting supervision is the best way to help insure a beneficial, safe experience.

▼ ▼ ▼ ▼ ▼

In the next chapter, you will learn about some of the many Natural Hygiene resources available to you!

▼ ▼ ▼ ▼ ▼ ▼ ▼ ▼ ▼

13

Natural Hygiene Resources

There are a great many resources available to you as you begin your new, healthier and happier lifestyle. Take advantage of these very special opportunities for you to grow in knowledge, experience, and enjoyment.

American Natural Hygiene Society

The American Natural Hygiene Society is the international center for current information and activities in the field of Natural Hygiene. Founded in 1948, the Society is the oldest and largest Natural Hygiene organization in the world, with more than 10,000 members in over 50 countries.

Largest Natural Hygiene organization in the world!

In fulfilling its mission, the Society has created many publications, programs, and services to promote its lifesaving message and empower people to choose true health independence for themselves and their loved ones.

The Society publishes the award-winning *Health Sci-*

ence magazine; conducts International Natural Living Conferences and Seminars; publishes and distributes Natural Hygiene books and tapes; and operates the Herbert Shelton Library (an historical library tracing the history of Natural Hygiene to its origin in the 1830s).

Join the American Natural Hygiene Society today!

Take advantage of the tremendous support system membership in the American Natural Hygiene Society brings.

Great membership benefits!

Membership benefits include:
1. A subscription to the Society's colorful, award-winning membership journal—*Health Science* magazine
2. Discounts on all ANHS Conferences and Seminars
3. Free ANHS book and tape catalog
4. Discounts on all books, audiotapes, and videotapes
5. List of Hygienic physicians who are members of the International Association of Hygienic Physicians
6. Membership card
7. Free member's decal for your car
8. ANHS Member Network, support groups, and more!

Annual membership dues are $25 in the United States, $45 in all other countries. To become a member or to get more information, contact:

American Natural Hygiene Society
P.O. Box 30630
Tampa, FL 33630
(813) 855-6607

Health Science magazine

Award ➨ winning magazine!

Health Science is the award-winning membership journal of the American Natural Hygiene Society. Published six times per year, this publication is the only major Natural Hygiene periodical published in the world today, with readers in over 50 countries.

Health Science includes interviews with the world's foremost physicians and teachers of Natural Hygiene, as well as recipes, diet tips, and articles on how to build and maintain exuberant health and a joyful lifestyle.

A one-year subscription to *Health Science* is $25 in the United States, $45 in all other countries.

To subscribe, contact:

> ***Health Science* magazine**
> **P.O. Box 30630**
> **Tampa, FL 33630**
> **(813) 855-6607**
>
> *Note: Members of the American Natural Hygiene Society (see opposite page) receive* ***Health Science*** *as part of their membership benefits.*

"I'm so glad you like it. Actually it's just sodium acid pyrophosphate, erythorbate, and glucono delta lactone with some meat flavoring."

ANHS on the Internet

Visit the American Natural Hygiene Society's Home Page on the World Wide Web. The Internet is a great way to get information about ANHS, and it is an easy way to introduce people to Natural Hygiene—just give them the ANHS Internet address: www.anhs.org.

ANHS Member Network

Members of the American Natural Hygiene Society who want to meet new friends and correspond with other members from around the world can request a free listing in the ANHS Member Network directory, which is published in each issue of *Health Science* magazine.

To become a member of the Society, see page 127.

ANHS International Natural Living Conferences and Seminars

Meet new friends from around the world while learning how to take control of your life and health!

Each year, the American Natural Hygiene Society conducts a five-day International Health Conference. The featured speakers are expert physicians from around the world who specialize in health, nutrition, exercise, prevention, rest, and recovery through natural methods.

These events have attracted thousands of people through the years. Taped recordings of the lectures and workshops have been distributed to thousands of others. The Society also conducts regional seminars.

For more information, contact the American Natural Hygiene Society. (See page 106.)

Natural Hygiene books and tapes

The American Natural Hygiene Society publishes and distributes thousands of books, audio, and videotapes on the subject of health and Natural Hygiene. The latest, most up-to-date and accurate information on Natural Hygiene is available on the Society's audio and videotapes. The Society publishes the best-selling book on fasting of all time, *Fasting Can Save Your Life,* by Herbert Shelton. To get a current catalog, contact the American Natural Hygiene Society. (See page 118.)

← All-time, best-selling book on fasting!

Herbert Shelton Library

The American Natural Hygiene Society maintains and operates the Herbert Shelton Library, an historical library which contains more than 2,000 books and periodicals on the subject of Natural Hygiene, dating back to the 1830s. This collection is of great value to university researchers with an interest in information on the history of Natural Hygiene.

The majority of the books and periodicals in the collection were written by medical doctors who abandoned their conventional practices in favor of Natural Hygiene. The collection is the largest of its kind in the world, and the only comprehensive source of historical information on Natural Hygiene.

If you have historical books on Natural Hygiene that you would like to donate to the Herbert Shelton Library, please contact the American Natural Hygiene Society. (See page 106.)

Other resources

The groups listed on the following pages fall into three categories: those that primarily base their ideas on the principles of Natural Hygiene, groups for physicians, and groups focusing on vegetarian nutrition and philosophy.

Professional associations:

International Association of Hygienic Physicians
204 Stambaugh Building
Youngstown, OH 44503
(330) 746-5000

IAHP is a professional association for licensed, primary-care physicians (medical doctors, osteopaths, chiropractors, and naturopaths) who provide Hygienic care. The IAHP offers an internship program for certification in fasting supervision. For more information on the IAHP, see Chapter 15.

Physicians Committee for Responsible Medicine
5100 Wisconsin Ave., NW, Suite 404
Washington, DC 20016
(202) 686-2210

PCRM publishes a newsletter, a vegetarian starter kit, and fact sheets on various aspects of health and nutrition.

"Well, then—two apples a day."

Natural Hygiene oriented groups:

Australian Natural Hygiene Society
Arcadia Health Center
Cobah Road, Arcadia NSW 2159 AUSTRALIA
61-2-653-1115
Publishes a newsletter and sponsors lectures and events.

British Natural Hygiene Society
Shalimar, Harold Grove
Frinton-On-Sea, Essex
CO13 9BD ENGLAND
441-25-567-2823
Publishes a newsletter and sponsors lectures and events.

Canadian Natural Health Association
439 Wellington St. W., #5
Toronto, Ontario, M5V 1E7 CANADA
(416) 977-2642
Publishes a newsletter and sponsors lectures and events.

Canadian Health Association
P.O. Box 92, Westmount Station
Westmount, Quebec, H3Z 2T1 CANADA
(514) 482-9736
Publishes a newsletter and sponsors lectures and events.

Natural Hygiene, Inc.
P.O. Box 2132 Huntington Station
Shelton, CT 06484
(203) 929-1557
Sponsors lectures, events, and a local radio program.

New Zealand Natural Hygiene Society
Omanawa, 24 Turere Place
Wanganui, Aotearoa, NEW ZEALAND
(06) 345-9394
Publishes a newsletter and sponsors lectures and events.

Vegetarian oriented groups:
(See next page.)

Vegetarian oriented groups:

American Vegan Society
56 Dinshah Lane, P.O. Box H
Malaga, NJ 08328
(609) 694-2887

Publishes a newsletter and sponsors events.

New Century Nutrition
P.O. Box 4716
Ithaca, NY 14852
(800) 841-0444

This group features the writing of world-renowned scientists, including T. Colin Campbell, Ph.D., of Cornell University, who is one of the most respected nutritional biochemists in the world. Publishes a newsletter, booklets, and recipe guides.

North American Vegetarian Society
P.O. Box 72
Dolgeville, NY 13329
(518) 568-7970

Publishes a newsletter and sponsors lectures and events.

Vegetarian Resource Group
P.O. Box 1463
Baltimore, MD 21203
(410) 366-8343

Publishes books and a journal and sponsors events in the Baltimore area.

▼ ▼ ▼ ▼ ▼

In the next chapter, learn how to get the best Natural Hygiene books, audiotapes, and videotapes!

▼ ▼ ▼ ▼ ▼ ▼ ▼ ▼ ▼

14

Natural Hygiene Books, Audiotapes, and Videotapes

The American Natural Hygiene Society offers a comprehensive collection of books, audiotapes, and videotapes on Natural Hygiene. The most important of them are listed here. To get a complete catalog of the books, audios, and videos available, see "Ordering Instructions" at the end of this chapter.

◂ *To order Natural Hygiene books and tapes, see p. 118!*

The most important current book for readers interested in Natural Hygiene is *Fasting and Eating For Health*, by Joel Fuhrman, M.D. Other historical classics, and up-to-date audio- and videotapes, are listed below.

Fasting and Eating For Health
Joel Fuhrman, M.D.   ***ANHS Book #230***
The most important book of its kind ever! Describes how fasting and aggressive nutritional changes can not only *prevent* disease but can actually *reverse* many serious illnesses. These recommendations for a natural diet are backed up by strong scientific documentation.   255 pp.

Natural Hygiene classics
To provide an in-depth look at the culmination of the first 100 years of thinking in Natural Hygiene, ANHS has

reprinted the seven best books by Dr. Herbert M. Shelton. These books, which were written between 20 and 60 years ago, offer a comprehensive description of Natural Hygiene of that period.

Books
The classic books on Natural Hygiene

Best-selling fasting book of all time! →

Fasting Can Save Your Life
Dr. Herbert M. Shelton　　　　　　　　　　　　*ANHS Book #182*
Discusses the benefits of fasting in various acute and chronic diseases, including arthritis, colitis, heart disease, and more. It establishes the difference between the popular pseudo-fasts, such as juice or fruit diets, and true fasting, which is abstinence.　　　　　　　　　195 pp.

Natural Hygiene: The Pristine Way of Life
Dr. Herbert M. Shelton　　　　　　　　　　　　*ANHS Book #219*
Considered by many to have been the most important book on Natural Hygiene ever written! Describes the total Natural Hygiene system as seen from the author's many decades of experience.　640 pp.

Fasting For Renewal of Life
Dr. Herbert M. Shelton　　　　　　　　　　　　*ANHS Book #231*
Dr. Shelton had more experience in fasting supervision than any other physician. Some of the specifics of his recommendations have changed over time, but his basic message still rings true today!　　314 pp.

Health For the Millions
Dr. Herbert M. Shelton　　　　　　　　　　　　*ANHS Book #242*
Offers an introduction to the principles and practices of Natural Hygiene. Includes chapters on all facets of a healthful lifestyle, and particularly the role of diet and nutrition.　　　　　　　　　　314 pp.

The Science and Fine Art of Natural Hygiene
Dr. Herbert M. Shelton　　　　　　　　　　　　*ANHS Book #218*
Learn why Natural Hygiene is so different from the other so-called "healing systems." For many years, people considered this book to be the best introduction to Natural Hygiene!　　　　　　　　　　420 pp.

The Science and Fine Art of Food and Nutrition
Dr. Herbert M. Shelton　　　　　　　　　　　　*ANHS Book #007*
Discusses our nutritional needs, what nutrition is, and what, when, and how to eat. It examines fruitarianism, vegetarianism, food combining, raw foods, the feeding of children, and more.　　　　591 pp.

The Science and Fine Art of Fasting
Dr. Herbert M. Shelton   **ANHS Book #006**
The most comprehensive book available on fasting. Dr. Shelton conducted over 40,000 fasts. There are more than 55 years of study, observation, and experiences accumulated in this remarkable book. Much of this information is not available elsewhere!   384 pp.

Dictionary of Natural Foods
William Esser, N.D.   **ANHS Book #017**
One of the best-selling books on the Natural Hygiene diet. Learn the exact nutrients of all the natural foods—everything you need to know in alphabetical order. Beautiful color photographs, food combining tips, food preparation, exotic fruits, and much more!   166 pp.

To order a book, see "Ordering Information" at the end of this chapter.

Audiotapes

These audiotapes, recorded at annual ANHS International Conferences, provide the most current Natural Hygiene information available!

Complete Set of 24 ANHS Conference Tapes
Speakers at ANHS International Conferences   **ANHS Audio #(by year)**
Lectures from the annual ANHS International Conferences offer the most comprehensive, up-to-date information on Natural Hygiene available. Topics range from the principles of Natural Hygiene to diet, stress management, the role of rest and sleep in the healing process, and how to put your total health program into practice.

◄ *The best way to get the facts about Natural Hygiene!*

Women's Health Issues *(six tapes)*
Drs. N. Burton, Fuhrman, Sabatino   **ANHS Audio #9751**
Topics include: Health Concerns of Women; Preventing and Reversing Arthritis and Osteoporosis; Understanding Your Hormones; Successful Weight Management; Women's Health Problems—Breast and Ovarian Cancer; and Facts and Myths about Aging.

What Is Natural Hygiene *(six tapes)*
Drs. A. Burton, N. Burton, Cridland, Goldhamer,
Sabatino; and J. M. Lennon   **ANHS Audio #9752**
Topics include: Hygienic Approach to Wellness—Maximizing Human Potential; Scientific Basis of Hygiene; Health Care vs. Disease Care; New Perspectives on the Principles and Practices of Natural Hygiene; Stress—The Hygienic Factor; and How to Be a Good Teacher of Natural Hygiene.

Fasting For Health *(six tapes)*
Drs. A. Burton, Cinque, Fuhrman, Goldhamer, Scott ANHS Audio #9753
Topics include: Fasting and Its Benefits; Fasting and Eating for Health—Validation by Modern Research; Dramatic Recoveries and Realistic Expectations in Fasting; How and When to Fast; How to Have a Successful Fast; The Importance of Living Healthfully after a Fast.

Diet and Nutrition *(six tapes)*
***Drs. Campbell, Cinque, Goldhamer, Klaper;
and V. Moran***   ***ANHS Audio #9754***
Topics include: Benefits of the Hygienic Diet; Benefits of a Plant-Based, Whole Food Diet; Tailoring the Natural Hygiene Diet to Meet Your Needs; Role of Diet in Health and Disease; Get the Fat Out; and Understanding the Science behind Vegetarian Nutrition.

To order audiotapes, see "Ordering Information" at the end of this chapter.

Videotapes
Some of the most important lectures at ANHS Conferences

Fabulous Food Festival
Joy Gross   ***ANHS Video #304***
The best party food video ever! Entertaining, creative approach to serving natural gourmet party foods. Festive and delicious ideas!

Feeding Healthy Families
Paula Duvall   ***ANHS Video #305***
Exciting new ways to prepare meals sure to please your family! Great tips and nutritional information from an experienced gourmet chef!

Understanding the Science behind Vegetarian Nutrition
Michael Klaper, M.D.   ***ANHS Video #306***
Up-to-date documentation of why the vegetarian diet works! Get the facts you need to stay healthy. A powerful and entertaining video!

The New Four Food Groups
Neal Barnard, M.D.   ***ANHS Video #307***
The New Four Food Groups is the way America will eat in the future! Understand why from the man who dared to challenge the meat myth!

Health Care of the Future
Joel Fuhrman, M.D.   ***ANHS Video #308***
Learn the way of future health care *now* before it's too late! Protect yourself and your family from out-of-date concepts. Offers a powerful look at your real health options!

Women's Health Issues
Nejla Burton, D.O.   *ANHS Video #309*

Powerful information that every woman needs to know to make wise choices in today's world! An eye-opening look at the way women are exploited by conventional "health" care!

Energy: The Key to Health
Ronald G. Cridland, M.D.   *ANHS Video #310*

Considered to be among some of the most important information presented in many years. Learn about the *vital* role that rest and sleep play in maintaining high-level health.

Fasting: Regeneration and Rejuvenation
Alec Burton, M.Sc., D.O., D.C.   *ANHS Video #311*

Learn the incredible benefits of a properly conducted fast from a leading world expert!

The Hygienic Approach to Wellness
Frank Sabatino, D.C., Ph.D.   *ANHS Video #312*

How to maximize your potential and experience personal transformation! Achieve total wellness!

Strategies for Healthful Living
Alan Goldhamer, D.C.   *ANHS Video #314*

Learn how to empower yourself to live the life you have always wanted! Learn the four basic principles and how to put them into practice in your life. Knowing what to do is just the first step.

Current Research in Support of Hygiene
Jennifer Marano, D.C.   *ANHS Video #315*

Learn how science continues to confirm the basic principles and the practices of Natural Hygiene! Your family and friends ask tough questions; here are the *answers*.

The Role of Diet in Health and Disease
Alan Goldhamer, D.C.   *ANHS Video #316*

Learn why what you eat plays a major role in your overall health. Your eating choices play an important part in how you feel! Learn how to live healthfully and happily from one of the most dynamic speakers in Natural Hygiene.

The Psychology of a Healthy and Happy Life
Douglas Lisle, Ph.D.   *ANHS Video #317*

Our emotions and well-being are directly related to how we think. A healthy and happy life begins with good mental choices. Learn how you can take steps that lead to health and happiness!

Cancer and Diabetes: Recognition and Resolution
Joel Fuhrman, M.D.   *ANHS Video #318*

Learn why the Hygienic lifestyle offers the best approach to prevention and care for these common diseases! Diet and lifestyle play an important role in these conditions!

Health Concerns of Seniors
Philip Martin, D.C.   *ANHS Video #319*

Learn how to design a successful health program and to overcome many of the so-called "problems of aging." Learn how to achieve dynamic wellness and fitness at any age!

Successful Weight Management: Why Diets Fail
Frank Sabatino, D.C., Ph.D.   *ANHS Video #320*

Learn how a totally healthful eating program promotes good health and successful weight management. Learn why diets fail and why the body tries to maintain its current weight!

Forever Young, Forever Healthy, Forever Beautiful
Keki Sidhwa, N.D., D.O.   *ANHS Video #321*

Learn how to apply the philosophy and principles of Natural Hygiene to live a wonderful and beautiful life! Learn how to create a magnificent life filled with light, beauty, and love.

Common Ailments: A Natural Hygiene Perspective
Alec Burton, M.Sc., D.O., D.C.   *ANHS Video #322*

Learn the importance of identifying and removing the causes of common health problems rather than treating the symptoms!

The Benefits of a Plant-Based, Whole-Food Diet
T. Colin Campbell, Ph.D.   *ANHS Video #323*

This world-renowned researcher presents dramatic, *documented* evidence to support recommendations to eat a plant-based, whole-food diet. An extraordinary look at information you will not see elsewhere.

Ordering Information

How to order books and tapes! → To order ANHS books, audiotapes, or videotapes with your VISA or MasterCard, please call (813) 855-6607, or fax (813) 855-8052, or E-mail anhs@anhs.org. Ordering hours are: 10am–4pm Mon.–Fri. Or write for a catalog: ANHS, P.O. Box 30630, Tampa, FL 33630.

▼ ▼ ▼ ▼ ▼

In the next chapter, you will learn all about the International Association of Hygienic Physicians.

15

Physicians in Natural Hygiene

Although Natural Hygiene is primarily a system of lifestyle management that leads to high-level health, its principles are equally effective in recovering from a wide variety of illnesses.

In a nutshell, there is a unity of health and disease, which means that people who are sick have the same basic needs as people who are well. However, they may need to modify their lifestyle, permanently or temporarily, to accommodate their individual limitations and capacities.

For example, all people have a need for movement and activity, but a person who is very old, frail, exhausted, or injured will not have the same exercise program as a person who is young, healthy, and vigorous.

In the case of illness, a person's activities may need to be extensively modified, and he or she may need to be under the supervision of a physician. Fortunately, there is an international association of licensed doctors, from a variety of disciplines, who can provide Hygienic care for patients.

Professional Natural Hygiene care

International Association of Hygienic Physicians

The International Association of Hygienic Physicians (IAHP) is a professional association for licensed, primary-care physicians (medical doctors, osteopaths, chiropractors, and naturopaths) who provide Hygienic care. Founded in 1978, the IAHP offers an internship program for certification in fasting supervision.

Membership is open to all licensed physicians—medical doctors, chiropractors, osteopaths, and naturopaths—who have graduated from a bona fide, accredited professional school. If you are a licensed physician or a stu-

"It may very well bring about immortality, but it will take forever to test it."

dent in one of those disciplines, and would like more information about the IAHP, contact Mark A. Huberman, IAHP, 204 Stambaugh Bldg., Youngstown, OH 44503; (330) 746-5000.

Hygienic physicians around the world

The following primary-care physicians are all licensed and/or legally practicing in their state, country, or territory and are members in good standing of the IAHP.

IAHP physicians agree to accept and abide by the Association's Principles of Ethics and Standards of Practice. Those listed as Certified members include the founders of the Association and those subsequent members who have successfully completed an internship (or its equivalent) in Hygienic care with an emphasis on fasting supervision, and are certified by the IAHP as Specialists in the Application of Fasting Supervision and Hygienic Care. This is the complete list of Hygienic Physicians at the time of publication.

United States

Northeast

Certified Members
Joel Fuhrman, M.D.
450 Amwell Rd., Belle Mead, NJ 08502; Phone: (908) 359-1775

Stanley S. Bass, D.C.
3119 Coney Island Ave., Brooklyn, NY 11235; Phone: (718) 648-1500

Non-certified Members
Thomas K. Hand, D.C.
3676 Richmond Ave., Staten Island, NY 10312; Phone: (718) 984-5869

Midwest

Certified Members
D.J. Scott, D.C.
Scott's Natural Health Institute
17023 Lorain Ave., Cleveland, OH 44111; Phone: (216) 671-5023

Roger Walker, D.C.
215 Ramsey St., Hastings, MN 55033; Phone: (612) 437-1876

IAHP members (continued)

South

Certified Members

William Esser, N.D., D.C.
Esser's Health Ranch
P.O. Box 6229, Lake Worth, FL 33466; Phone: (407) 965-4360

Frank Sabatino, D.C., Ph.D.
Regency House Natural Health Spa
2000 S. Ocean Drive, Hallandale, FL 33009; Phone: (954) 454-2220

John Brosious, D.C. *(retired)*
18209 Gulf Blvd., Redington Shores, FL 33708; Phone: (813) 392-8326

Robert Sniadach, D.C.
11211 S. Military Trail, Suite 4923, Boynton Beach, FL 33436; Phone: (561) 369-8040

David Aukamp, D.C.
5060 Sunrise Lane, Cumming, GA 30131; Phone: (770) 933-7725

Non-certified Members

Steven P. Nelson, D.C.
12551 Indian Rocks Rd., Suite 2, Largo, FL 34644; Phone: (813) 460-4221

Southwest

Certified Members

Ralph C. Cinque, D.C.
Dr. Cinque's Health Retreat
305 Verdin Dr., Buda, TX 78610; Phone: (512) 295-4256

West

Certified Members

Alan Goldhamer, D.C.
Jennifer Marano, D.C.
David Engle, D.C.
Alec Isabeau, D.C.
Erwin Linzner, D.C.
Center for Conservative Therapy
4310 Lichau Rd., Penngrove, CA 94951; Phone: (707) 792-2325

Ronald G. Cridland, M.D.
Health Promotion Clinic
6010 Commerce Boulevard., #152, Rohnert Park, CA 94928; Phone: (707) 586-5555

Gerald Benesh, D.C.
2050 Rockhoff Rd., Escondido, CA 92026; Phone: (619) 747-4193

Charisse Basquin, D.C.
728 Gaffney, Fairbanks, AK 99701; Phone: (907) 456-6213

PHYSICIANS IN NATURAL HYGIENE ▼ 123

International

Australia
Certified Members
Nejla Burton, D.O., D.C.; Alec Burton, M.Sc., D.O., D.C.
Arcadia Health Centre
Cobah Road, Arcadia, N.S.W. 2159 AUSTRALIA; Phone: 011-61-2-653-1115

Douglas F. Evans, D.O.
19 Clay St., Balmain
New South Wales 2040, AUSTRALIA; Phone: 011-43-2-818-2165

Canada
Certified Members
Philip Martin, D.C.
15 Ridge Hill Dr., Toronto, Ontario, M6C 2J2 CANADA; Phone: (416) 785-9091

England
Certified Members
Keki R. Sidhwa, N.D., D.O.
Shalimar
Harold Grove, Frinton-on-Sea, Essex CO139BD ENGLAND; Phone: 011-441-25-567-2823

Germany
Non-certified Members
K.J. Probst, M.D.
Greuth 3, 87758 Kronburg GERMANY; Phone: 011-49-8394-1450

Now, of the 12 drugs we've tested on you, which one tasted best?"

IAHP members (continued)

Greece
Certified Members
Theodora Coumentakis, M.D.; Peter Coumentakis, N.D.
Palaion Polemiston 34, Glyfada, 16674, Athens, GREECE; Phone: 011-30-1-962-2387

Israel
Certified Members
Dan Keret, M.D.
69 Hahadarim St., Sede Warburg 44935 ISRAEL; Phone: 011-972-9-982-895

Non-certified Members
Dan Gur, D.O., N.D., M.R.O.
21 Tsiveoni St., Vardia, Haifa 34651 ISRAEL; Phone: 011-972-4-340138

Japan
Non-certified Members
Guy Harris, D.O.
Kamiuma 5-33-4, Setagaya-ku, Tokyo 154 JAPAN; Phone: 011-81-3-5430-3480

New Zealand
Non-certified Members
Nigel Brooke, N.D., D.O.; Amanda Brooke, D.O.
Omanawa, 24 Turere Place, Wanganui Aotearoa, NEW ZEALAND; Phone: 011-64-6-345-9394

A public service

The American Natural Hygiene Society has no direct or indirect financial interest in this list of physicians. ANHS does not diagnose, prescribe, or recommend any particular treatment or approach to any specific condition, but simply makes available the names and addresses of members of the International Association of Hygienic Physicians as a public service. In providing this information, ANHS assumes no responsibilities for fees charged, healthcare rendered, or guidance provided.

The American Natural Hygiene Society is a nonprofit, non-sectarian health organization dedicated to educating the public in the principles of Natural Hygiene.

▼ ▼ ▼ ▼ ▼

In the next chapter, you will learn how to become an American Natural Hygiene Society member!

16

Becoming an ANHS Member

Now that you have learned about all of the benefits of Natural Hygiene, we hope that you will want to become a member of the American Natural Hygiene Society (ANHS). In addition to all of the other benefits you will receive, ANHS membership can be a tremendous support system for you.

ANHS is the international center for current information and activities in the field of Natural Hygiene. Founded in 1948, the Society is the oldest and largest Natural Hygiene organization in the world, with more than 10,000 members in over 50 countries.

By becoming an ANHS member, you create a powerful partnership that brings tremendous benefits. You *receive* many tangible benefits—a subscription to the award-winning *Health Science* magazine; discounts on all ANHS Conferences and Seminars; discounts on Natural Hygiene books, audiotapes, and videotapes; ongoing updates about critical health issues, such as food irradiation and important legislation; and much more!

◂ *Valuable benefits!*

Your support makes a big difference! ➡

By being an ANHS member, you also *give* a tremendous gift. Your ongoing membership helps ANHS spread the lifesaving message of Natural Hygiene to people around the world. The support of knowledgeable, caring people like you can mean the difference between life and death for people who are suffering needlessly for lack of information.

Join the American Natural Hygiene Society today!

Take advantage of the tremendous support system membership in the American Natural Hygiene Society brings.

Membership benefits include:
1. A subscription to the Society's colorful, award-winning membership journal—*Health Science* magazine
2. Discounts on all ANHS Conferences and Seminars
3. Free ANHS book and tape catalog
4. Discounts on all books, audiotapes, and videotapes
5. List of Hygienic physicians who are members of the International Association of Hygienic Physicians
6. Membership card
7. Free member's decal for your car
8. ANHS Member Network, support groups, and more!

Annual membership dues are $25 in the United States, $45 in all other countries. To become a member or to get more information, contact:

American Natural Hygiene Society
P.O. Box 30630
Tampa, FL 33630
(813) 855-6607 (Voice)
(813) 855-8052 (Fax)
anhs@anhs.org (E-mail)

Become a member!
American Natural Hygiene Society
Living in harmony with Nature

Here are just 5 of the great reasons why you should become an ANHS member!

1. You'll receive a subscription to the Society's award-winning *Health Science* magazine!
2. Learn how to achieve your optimum weight...*naturally!*
3. Get discount prices on all of the many ANHS books, audiotapes, and videotapes!
4. Learn how to prepare delicious, nutritious meals!
5. Enjoy a happier, healthier life than you ever thought possible—and support a noble cause at the same time!

☑ YES! I want to become a member!

Enclosed are my membership dues.
☐ $25US ($45US outside USA and Canada)

Name: _____
Address: _____
City: _____ State _____ Zip: _____

Make checks payable to:
American Natural Hygiene Society
P.O. Box 30630, Tampa, FL 33630

Visit ANHS on the Internet: anhs.org
Contact us via E-mail: anhs@anhs.org